CRAZY things PARENTS text

CRAZY things PARENTS text

Laughing at the expense of your parent's texts

Stephen and Wayne Miltz

Published by Sourcebooks, Inc.

P.O. Box 4410, Naperville, Illinois 60567-4410

(630) 961-3900

Fax: (630) 961-2168

www.sourcebooks.com

Library of Congress Cataloging-in-Publication data is on file with the publisher.

Printed and bound in the United States of America.

VP 10 9 8 7 6 5 4 3 2 1

➡ contents

➡ introduction:
the seven phases
of textual maturity

This book is for every family that has ever dealt with immature parental texting. That's right, at the heart of it, it's for and about families. We may poke fun at parents a lot, but the truth is, it's only because we love their texts so darn much that they are so funny. We believe that the texting relationship has allowed parents and children to become closer, and we'll tell you why. Unfortunately though, we're not parents quite yet, so we can't really speak for them. So while we talk about what we've learned about parents and the text message, just remember, we are only giving our point of view because we've learned one thing above all else: we'll *never* know what is going on inside of our parents' heads, so we shouldn't try to assume. Instead, this is a tribute to parents who text everywhere. It's for our parents and our friends' parents. It's for all of the parents that have unknowingly had their texts posted on our website. Maybe it'll even be a guide for them to know "what not to do."

Take it for what it is, but this is what we have observed.

Parents. They were our best friends in elementary school, embarrassed us in middle school, and pissed us off in high school. Just when we thought we were getting away from them in college, cell phones came along and pulled us right back in. But then something weird happened: we started to kind of like talking to them—as long as we didn't have to talk to them.

Enter the text message.

All of a sudden we could bridge the gap between the "too-cool-for-school kid who never comes home" and the "move-on-already and stop talking to your parents every ten minutes kid." Slowly but surely, the wall between parent and child crumbled to the earth, and technology put mother and daughter, father and son, on the same footing. Maybe it's because we had to teach them how to use the damn phone in the first place, and so they were humbled to where they finally saw us as more than just a depository for their hard earned income—we could actually teach them something! Whatever it was, parents decided they could open up more if they didn't have to have a long conversation with you face to face, and vice versa.

Of course, it wasn't that easy. First, we had to put up with the half dialed texts, the texts with no spaces, the all caps texts, and the unreadably autocorrected texts that Mom and Dad didn't know how to fix. That was funny in and of itself, and pretty much provided hours of entertainment—

and frustration. But along with that frustration came an odd sense of fulfillment. We were somehow helping our poor, technologically inept parents, and humored them until they started to get the hang of it. We found texts like "Howdoyoutypeaspaceonthisdamnthing.goingtoseegrandma. studyhard" to be utterly endearing. At the risk of sounding hyperbolic, it actually brought us closer together.

Then things got weird.

Mom and Dad learned the basics and decided to venture out on their own, unsupervised. They thought, "Hey, this is fun with the kids. Let's do it with each other." Little did we know how ugly—and horrifying—that could get. They could type, but somehow they managed to only know how to send text messages to three or four people. You know, their immediate family. And sometimes, God knows how, they got those mixed up in their contacts. This wasn't such a bad thing when you got a text from your mom that said "Sweetheart, could you pick up some milk on your way home?" All you had to do was reply and say, "Mom, you meant to text dad. I'm 500 miles away at college."

But it was the "insexts" that caused the damage. You would be sitting in class, or at work, when all of sudden you get a text from your mom: "Hello clit commander. I've had a long day and need some hard lovin. Cum home fast and rock my world." Things just got less funny. And all of a sudden you and your parents were a hell of a lot closer for reasons you had not wanted, nor had you anticipated. Yet, again, you were closer nonetheless. Somehow, you began to understand you parents better, and they started to be able to treat you more like an adult as you viewed them as more of one, and not just your mom or dad.

And that's when it all fell apart. They knew everything: how to text, what we were doing, where we were, who we were with—the whole nine yards. Before we knew it, they became the masters. They knew all we did, plus had years of experience, wisdom, and practice at belittling people. They started playing with us. Ultimately, it became a game of wits. Pretty soon it turned in to this:

> **Dad:** You're 16, sex doesn't exist for you. It's not real, like the Easter Bunny.

> **Us:** And you are married. It doesn't exist for you either. Ha.

> **Dad:** Touche, son. Touche.

And that's how we learned that you can actually become equals with your parents by texting. Ironic, right? A device created to disallow verbal communication actually made us talk more, and talk more openly with our parents.

Our parents love us so much because they watched us grow up. Now, we've finally been lucky enough to see our parents mature before our eyes (textually speaking), instead of the other way around. You see, they were able to enjoy seeing us learn to talk, get the confidence to go out on our own and screw up royally—only to get back up and try again. They watched our embarrassment as they found dirty magazines or fancy underwear, suffered our "advice" as we found that we knew absolutely everything there was to know (the beautiful teenage years); then they put up with us talking back to them, and loved us anyway. We insulted them, and they loved us more. Then we all grew up and became friends.

But then those damn text messages came around, and our parents were technological infants. Then *WE* got the opportunity to love our parents by watching them grow up. For all intents and purposes, we've seen seven distinct phases of their textual development. For that reason, we've divided the book into the "Seven Phases of Textual Maturity" that just about each and every parent goes through before they are digitally and telephonically adept. True, some parents just get it right off the bat; but think about it, there were those kids that you went to high school with that could have been 35 years old, married, and had two kids, and you wouldn't have questioned it.

This book is for the everyman. It's for the parents who went through this process, and the kids that taught them. It's for all those that thought that "LOL" meant "Lot of Love" and couldn't type worth a damn. Most of all it's for families that text together.

So what do you say: enough with the emotional appeals? Well, the bottom line is that regardless of what the motivations are, parents can have some pretty damn crazy texts, whether they mean to or not. So, we made a website to showcase some of the best from all of you and your parents. We wrote this book to showcase some of the best that we held back from the website, and to explain a little more in depth why we created the site and what the texts really represent. But that's all touchy feely stuff that you may not care about. If you do, that's great. If you don't you'll still LOL, LMFAO, WTF, and JBYM when reading these texts.

So, with that, enjoy. And remember, kids, keep texting. And parents, keep texting crazy things. We love it, and it's made us love you more.

→ phase 1:
lost in translation

Before they walked—and eventually ran ahead of us—our parents crawled and limped into the world of texting. Like a fifteen-year-old boy trying to ask a girl out on their first date, it did not go well. But let's give them some credit, they didn't grow up with T9 and Touch-Tone phones. It would have been hard to text with a rotary. So we suffered through the illegible texts and laughed at their failures, because c'mon, it was pretty damn funny.

In retrospect, it's kind of like when parents videotape their kids when they first start talking and mix up the words or mispronounce them. These videos are hilarious and almost bring a tear to a parent's eye when they look back on them years later.

That's what these nascent-phase texts are like for us. We've videotaped the learning process of our parents and reproduced the cutest, funniest, and downright most off-the-wall texts our parents sent us. Enjoy, because when they grow up, they become resentful teenagers (we mean parents) who just talk back to us. So remember the days…

PERIODS

Dad: I.just.figured.out.how.to.text

Me: Great, now just remove those periods and you're set.

Dad: Thats.what.she.said

WHO SINGS THAT SONG

Mom: Who sings that song… something about tonight being a good night.

Mom: Black Guy Pees? Right?

LOUD MEXICANS...

Mom: HEY! HOW'S IT GOING?

Me: Mom, you know that when you're texting in all caps it means that you're yelling right...

Mom: YEAH, I KNOW IM AT WALMART AND THERE ARE A BUNCH OF LOUD MEXICANS RUNNING AROUND SO I HAVE TO YELL FOR YOU TO HEAR ME

FLIRTY FACE FOR DAD

Mom: I made a new flirty face for dad!!!!!!!

Me: ok...? I'll see it when I get to the house

Mom: It's like this ;{B (my upper lip and teeth).

Me: that's horrifying.

IRON MAIDEN

Mom: Hey, I need to borrow a pair of those really high heel Iron Maiden shoes you have.

Me: Maybe you mean those by Steve Madden.

FOUNDATION OFFICE

Mom: f off

Me: huh? what did i do???

Mom: oops i meant im waiting for you at the Foundation OFFice.

DEATH OF A TEXTMAN

Me: I can't talk anymore dad, my phone is dying :(

Dad: CPR!!

VOICE MAIL

Mom: I got an upside down pair of sunglasses, with a 2 next to it...but I can't find anything I have not yet opened. Any clue?

Me: I have NO IDEA what you're talking about.

Mom: On the bar on the top line of my phone where it tells me I have messages.

Me: Voicemail, Mom. Voicemail.

FORNICATING ANTS

ME: These ants are fucking everywhere!!!!

MOM: Are they using protection?

STFU

Mom: what does 'stfu' mean?

Me: it means shut the fuck up...

Mom: oh i thought it meant 'should try for you,' because i sent your dad a text asking him to try to clean the garage and he told me 'stfu'.

SHRUGGED

Me: Dad what time do you want me home?

Dad: Shrugged

NEW PHONE

Mom: Hi. I just got a new phone.

Me: Cool! What's it like?

Mom: Hard

JERSEY SHORE MIX-UP

Me: So my friends decided that I'm going to be called Jwoww from now on.

Mom: Oh, I don't know her. I only know Snootchie and the Scenario.

SPEED DIAL

Me: You called momma?

Mom: Not really. just checkin the time walking the pup. Accidentally hit the speed dial. Was wondering how u r.

RIBZ

Dad: on da way home wit da ribz!

Me: Where did you learn to talk like that?

Dad: songs on the radio

CAPS PLEASE

FROM DAD:

Please use caps im having
trouble hearing

AUTHOR NOTE:
This is something our dad would say. He actually uses
the app that reads texts out loud in a robot voice

S.L.U.T

Me: Hey I'm gonna stay at Davids
tonight. Love Mere

Mom: S.L.U.T

Me: WHAT?

Mom: So Love You Too

GTD

Mom: R u home yet? need U 2 GTD

Me: Mom, what the hell does GTD mean?

Mom: GET THE DISHWASHER!

Me:...Oh okay. You know, you can't just go around making your own acronyms.

FAXER

Me: Is Heather alive? She hasn't responded to any of my texts for a week

Dad: Maybe her faxer is broke

LADY HAHA

FROM GRANDPA:

I just saw Lady Haha
on the grammys. i don't
understand the appeal. I
just love Justin Beeber!

MOM'S FIRST TEXT

FROM MOM:

Hi Honey. I AM MOM.

MYSPACE

Me: I thought the picture turned out cute.

Mom: Are you gonna put it on Yourspace?

GRAB SOMEBODY

Dad: Grab somebody sexy and tellem "HEY"!

Me: excuse me?

Dad: Enrique and I just wanted to say Hello!

THE LAZY TEXTER

Me: Can I go to Adam's house?

Dad: y

Me: ...because I wanna hang out with my friends

Dad: y

Me: ......because it's fun.

Dad: y = yes

Me: ...I'll just call you next time

MOM THAT'S BACKWARD

FROM MOM:

Your brother just taught
me how to make a dong
with texting! D====8

GET HIS NUMBER

DAD: Hey, do you have Ian's number?

ME: No.

DAD: You should text him and ask him for it.

WHO IS SHE?

Me: Come on daddd. It's not my fault, they're making me late!

Dad: Dont come on me! Come on your friends!

Me: That's what she said

Dad: Who is she?

LUCKY

Me: Happy Birthday Dad! Did you get anything good?

Dad: Yep

Me: What did you get?

Dad: Lucky

TTUL

Mom: Ok. Luv u. Ttul

Me: Mom, it's ttyl

Mom: Oh. Well I like u better, its easier!

J SQUARED

Dad: Free breakfast at chick-fil-a all month!

Me: I know, my friends and I are going all week!

Dad: I am j squared epically

Me: Excuse me?

Dad: I am really jealous.

EBONICS APP

Me: Got my report card!

Dad: better b all As or ill pop a cap in yo ass

Me: Purchasing the ebonics guide for your ipad was the worst thing ive ever let you do

Dad: word

TWIT PIC

Mom: I saw your twat pic you posted it was cute

Me: What?

Mom: Isn't that what you said pictures on Twitter were called?

TRYING 2 BE HIP

Dad: WHEN U FINNA B HOME?

Me: Why do you text in all caps? Did you mean to say "finna?"

Dad: BCUZ IM TRYING 2 BE HIP

ROLLING PAPERS

Mom: What's with the rolling papers you left on the table?

Me: I don't know what your talking about

Mom: The ones in the avon case

Me: Those are oil removing face strips.

Mom: Sure.

BREAKING UP

Me: Hi mom!

Mom: My phones breaking up, can't hear you.

TYPING WITH MY PENIS

Dad: Hih

Me: hey

Dad: oopsd soirry im realy bad at typinf witg my penisa

Me: WHAT!?!?!?

Dad: you heardf me

CHEESE STICK

Dad: I'm listening to this like a cheese stick song. Its annoying. It keeps coming on the radio

Me: I think you mean like a G6...

Dad: nope its cheese stick

AUTHOR NOTE:
It is amazing what parents think the lyrics to songs are these days. Our mom thought the lyrics to Jeremiah's "Birthday Sex" was "Birthday Text!"

SOUTHAMPTON

Me: Mom! I just saw Paris Hilton walking around Southampton!!

Mom: Do you think she just texted all her friends that she saw you??

THEY WERE HOT?

Me: The Celtics were really having trouble with the heat.

Mom: They were too hot?

Me: No the Miami heat

Mom: They couldn't get out of the heat?

Me: Really?.....

BUT I WANT THE INTERNET

Me: Just go to google and type in "recipe."

Aunt: Oh honey i dont want google, i want the internet.

I FORGOT

Mom: Our internet is down, but don't worry I am on it.

Me: Ok mom, what happened?

Mom: HOW DID YOU GET THIS MESSAGE?!

Mom: Oh wait, I forgot texting isn't hooked to the internet...

YOUR LAPTOP IS A THIEF

Mom: I think it might be sucking the Wi-Fi out of my phone.

Me: What is?

Mom: Your laptop.

COST EXTRA?

Me: You and Dad have fun on your trip!

Mom: Can you email over the ocean? Or does that cost extra?

<3

FROM MOM:

John just less than 3 me
:)

RETRO

Mom: This party is super groovy wish you were here!!

Me: Wow mom your old no one says groovy anymore.

Mom: i'm not old....Just happily RETRO!!!

PIMPING YOUR RIDE

I heard about this "vagazzles" thing? Is it like...pimping your ride?

BETTY LOW

Mom: I think I keep getting messages or missed calls or something.

Me: From who?

Mom: Some woman called...Betty Low?

Me: Umm BATTERY LOW???

Mom: Yeah thats it!

OH GRANDPA

Dad: Your Grandpa took a dump in a customers front yard.

Me: HE DID WHAT?!

Dad: He was walking to the van and he tripped on some cement.

Me: ...and shit himself?

Dad: What no whats wrong with you?

SPACES

Me: Why do you put spaces between every letter?

Dad: h o w d i d y o u d o t h a t w i t h o u t a l l t h e s p a c e s

WHERE IS MY DROID?

Dad: Where is my Droid.

Me: In your hand if you're texting me.

Dad: Right. Carry on.

WITH ALL MY

FROM ME:

i love you with all my butt.... i would say heart but my butt is bigger

A JOKE

Dad: Want to hear a joke?

Me: Ok

Dad: Sex.

Me: I don't get it...

Dad: Hahahaha, of course you don't get it.

CRACKALACKALACKING

Mom: What's Crackalackalacking?

Me: Where did you learn that?

Mom: The Snoopy Dog guy on TV

BURNED

Dad: How did i get such a beautiful daughter?

Me: The Mailman

Dad: OHHHH BURN! ;D

Me: O.o

ROFLMAO

Mum: Whats ROFLMAO? Is it Rolling Around With My Fists In My Arse?

Me: It is now

WTF?

Dad: What does WTF mean?

Me: What the fuck.

Dad: WATCH YOUR LANGUAGE LITTLE LADY OR I WILL KICK YOU INTO NEXT WEEK

FILM

Mom: My digital camera doesn't have enough film in it?

Me: shah digital cameras don't use film.

Mom: Well, it doesn't have enough digitals?

FROM MOM:

Your DVD is sitting
on the table. Sorry I
couldn't figure out how
to rewind it :(

HEADBANDS

Dad: Have you noticed that ninjas
and sushi makers have the same
headbands.

Me: ...

Dad: Might have found the ninjas
hideout :)

A SNAKE

Mom: What does D: mean

Me: Its a sad face. Look at it backwards

Mom: Ohhh I see _____^^_____*~

Me: What is that?

Mom: A Snake that ate an M! :)

Me: ...No Mom. Just no

PENTHOUSE APARTMENT!

Me: I cant believe he proposed with a ring AND the keys to a c!!!

Dad: Thats my girl,,, I always knew you would sleep your way to the top just not literally to the top of the building

PHOTO

Mom: You give me photo now.

Me: What are you, Asian?

BOMBDIGGITY

Mom: hey sweetie how'd the test go?

Me: Good! I got a 95% on it

Mom: Oh That's the bombdiggity!!!

Me: Omg mom the only thing hip about you is a hip replacement.

DID I GET IT RIGHT?

Me: What are you doing?

Dad: Your Mom!

Me: !! :O

Dad: So is that sexting?

NAKED

Mom

Do you want me to get Naked for you?

Sick...Umm idk how to respond to that mom

OH! im at Costco, I meant that Naked drink you like so much!

NEMO

FROM MOM:

He was one of those
people who wear black
tight keens. with that
weird hair that covers
one eye. You know....Nemo

MOZZARELLA

FROM MOM:

So I open mozzarella
Firefox, then what?

BUMPER STICKER

Dad: What does DTF mean?

Me: Down To Fight, of course

Dad: Perfect. Got a DTF sticker for my car.

DEFINE STUPID

Dad: Can't find my phone anywhere.

Me: Seems like you have another problem

Dad: Whats that?

Me: Some dude stole it and is texting me off it.

Dad: D:< Who?

Me: Just someone really Stupid…

BYE!

Mom: 10 4

Me: a simple "bye" would work...

Mom: but it's not as fun. XXX

ARE YOU LISTENING

Dad: Make sure you pick up your brother after school.

Dad: DID YOU HEAR ME?

Me: No.

Dad: LIMM

Me: Huh?

Dad: "Laughing in my mind" I wanted to make up one of my own

FOR A SECOND THERE...

FROM DAD:

--v^---v^---v^_____v^---
v^--- For a second there,
I was bored to death!

HOW TO

Mom: How do you send a text again?

Me:.......

IN WHAT CONTEXT

Mom: Hey what does this mean? (.)(.)

Me: in what context

Mom: I'm In love with ur (.)(.)

Me: ummm, EYES. Dad loves your eyes.

Mom: awww that's cute!

Me: Be sure to tell him you enjoy his 8--D Smile

→ phase 2:
i meant to send that to your father...

Ok, so our parents learned to type. They understood the value and convenience of the text message, began using it regularly, and thought it was fun. Unfortunately, they didn't fully understand the process. They could type well enough, but they only had three contacts in their phone: son, daughter, spouse. We don't know why, and we don't know how, but those three contacts became a game of Russian Roulette, and you never knew who was going to get a text intended for the wrong person. Your sister started getting texts intended for you, your brother starting getting texts intended for your dad, and so on and so on. Some of these were annoying, some of them were cute. But some of them were just fucking disturbing.

You had your run of the mill wrong numbers. Then you had the unintentional texts that were complaining about someone who accidentally ended up receiving that very text message. Awkward. The attempts at recovering from those are priceless.

And then, there was wrong number that introduced the point of no return. Remember, parents, when you first recognized us taking longer showers, hiding dirty magazines, or God forbid walked in on us discovering our sexuality? You had to come to terms with the fact that we were burgeoning adults who were going to have sexual desires at some point. You did NOT want to face that.

Well parents, we've got news for you: neither do kids. We don't want to walk in on our parents having sex, and we don't want to think of them as anything but our parents: not sexually active adults, not horny husbands, not seductive wives. And we definitely don't want to get "insexted."

What are insexts? Those sexts that your mom meant to send to your dad, your dad meant to send to a friend about your mom, or vice versa. Or even ones you meant to send to your friends, but sent to a parent instead.

We have a hard time laughing at these if they happened to us, but you've got to admit: when it happens to someone else it's pretty damn funny. So enjoy the best of crazythingsparentstext .com's wrong numbers and accidental insexts at the expense of others. Just don't think of your own parents when you read them…

DELETE THIS NOW

Mom: The sex last night was great. You made my body feel amazing ;)

Me: Mom…?

Mom: Delete this now

ROLE PLAY NIGHT

Dad: honey where did you put our dilldo's?

Me: WHATTTT?

Dad: oh sorry i ment to text your mom tonight is role playing night ;)

I HAVE AN ITCH

Mom: i have an itch in the back of my throat, you have anything for it? ;)

Me: ....mom?

Mom: oh dear lord, that was for your father

DID YOU WIN?

Mom: I can't wait until you get home from the game because I have a naughty surprise for you ;)

Me: MOM!!! WTF!! This is your son!!

Mom: OMG hi honey did you win your game?

LOST RING

Dad: I think my wedding ring was lost when my hand was up there. Do you think you could look for it for me?

Me: OH GOD, DAD.

Dad: DAMN IT.

Dad: I accidentally texted Daniel about this. I think my ring is in your pussy from last night.

Me: Dad, I'm getting a new number.

BEST I'VE EVER HAD

Me: I swear you're the best I've ever had...

Mom: Honey, keep it in your pants. If you're like your father you only lasted 5 minutes.

Me: OMG MOM REALLY?!?!?!?!?!

BIEBER FEVER

Dad: Where are you?

Me: At the Justin Bieber movie premiere DUH!

Dad: Like oh my gawwddd have a good time.

Me: wow Dad...you just killed it...

YOURS DEFINITELY WINS

Me: I was Spiderman and I saved her. Then we had sex on a rooftop.

Dad: My first sex dream, I blew myself. Yours definitely wins.

Me: Dad, My friend stole my phone that wasn't me

Dad: Really? My friend did too.

Dad: Should I pick up lube or will you?

Me: DAD, WHAT?!

Dad: LUKE! I mean Luke your Brother...nevermind I will just get him

Me: Get a new phone I don't need any more heart attacks.

TODAY'S BIG DEAL

Me: Time to get up and suck today's BIG DICK!

Dad: What time should I expect you.

Me: Sent that to the wrong person...

THE ONLY REASON

Mom: Is it sad that the only reason I haven't lapsed into depression is that I'm prettier than her?

Me: Who mom?

Mom: Sorry honey...I thought I texted Jill. But your father has a new girlfriend.

GRADE A LOVING

Mom: You comin home early today for some grade a loving (;

Me: Mom...WTF?

Mom: Shit that was supposed to go to your dad. Forward it to him for me. Thanks cutie!

AUTHOR NOTE:
It's amazing how many of these kind we get. Thankfully, it's never happened with our parents though. Please DO NOT LET THIS BE A JINX!

TUESDAY FUN NIGHT

Me: Staying at a friend's tonight

Mom: the little ones going to a friend's tonight, want to have a Tuesday date night...or should i say... Tuesday fun night? *wink wink*

Me: MOM !?!?!?!?!?

Mom: oops that was supposed to go to your dad...

ROSES ARE RED...

Dad: Roses are red, poems are corny, the way you go down on me makes me so horny. Sex Tonight?

Me: gross...Dad...Please tell me this was for mom

Dad: Oh no! I'm embraced! Sorry honey

Me: Scarred. For. Life

COMMANDER MOM

Mom: Clit-commander five mins till I'm home!

Me: Mom? this is your son.

Mom: Hey honey was ur day honey?

Me: ...Nevermind

Mom: Tom I accidentally sex texted our son!

Me: MOM WTF?

I'M MOVING OUT

Mom: Where is the Vibrator? Either you come NOW, or tell me where it is!

Me: Uhhhhh…MOM?? I think you may have scarred me for life!

Mom: Oh Sorry! Its not what you think we have code names, vibrator means soap

Mom: Jon, I accidentally toted Sara, Thought it was you. Where is the vibrator?

Me: Really? Im moving out.

YOU'RE IN HIGH SCHOOL!

Me: I know I was blacked out but apparently I looked fiercely at the toilet and said "we meet again"

Mom: You were what? You're in High School come home now we need to have a talk.

BOOBS FOR WATER

Dad

Dad: We had to leave the bar because you were trying to show the bartender your boobs for water.

Me: I think you meant to send that to Mom...No wonder she hasn't gotten out of bed today.

Send

FIND SOMEONE LIKE YOUR MOM TO MARRY

Dad: Yesterday was great she greeted me wearing a New York Yankees jersey and gave me an opening day blowjob.

Me: Umm excuse me?

Dad: Sorry son…all I have to say is find someone like your mom to marry.

WORSE WAYS

Dad: Well, there are worse ways to make $50 at a gay club.

Me: Umm Dad???

CHEATING

Dad: Ok, the bar is closing do I go home to my wife or my girlfriend?

Me: You better be going home to Mom....Are you seriously cheating on her? Please tell me this was a joke you meant to send to one of your stupid friends.

MY PARENTS BED

Me: somethin' about having sex in my parents bed makes me feel like I'm finally an adult.

Dad: When you get home I'm gonna whoop your ass.

WAITING FOR SOMEONE TO UNWRAP ME

Mom: Sitting here dressed up like a present waiting for someone to unwrap me ;)

Me: UMMM MOM GROOO....Is that why you were all excited I was spending the night out?

THIS IS YOUR DAUGHTER

Dad: I want to see you every morning in the kitchen ass naked in heels making waffles.

Me: Stop sending me these texts. This is your daughter not your girlfriend.

FREAK FLAG

Dad: I just accidentally walked in on our son and his girlfriend having sex and I was right!!! She had her freak flag flying high!

Me: Dad did you and mom seriously have a talk about my girlfriend being a freak?

AUTHOR NOTE:
No words. Just. No. Words.

APRIL FOOLS

Mom: Honey our daughter just noticed the "toothpaste" stain on my shirt...she kept trying to get it off by licking her thumb and rubbing it. I didn't know how to stop her

Me: MOM DID YOU SERIOUSLY LET ME LICK Dad's "Toothpaste"

Mom: April Fools???

Me: Not April. Im moving out

AUTHOR NOTE:
I hope for the kid's sake that he is also a personal trainer...

GOD'S WAY

Mom: it's like his penis is God's way of saying "sorry about his face"

Me: OMG Mom. What the Hell?

Mom: I thought I was responding to your aunt's text…

Me: No, I asked how your day was going.

BENEFITS

Me: Should I feel bad that my boyfriend pays for my birth control and his friends get to reap the benefits?

Mom: WHAT? Momma didn't raise no whore. Come home NOW.

Me: I meant to text ashley that. It was just a joke anyways.

Mom: Momma is no fool either.

SAD MASTURBATION

Mom: I fell asleep with my vibrator still in me. I am the Queen of Sad Masturbation.

Mom: Please Delete...

Mom: Honey?

Mom: I promise that wasn't meant for you...and you know I have been having a hard time since your father and I split.

AUTHOR NOTE:
Don't know whether to feel horrified or depressed. Or both.

I'M NOT A DAD!

Me: Joe looked down at his phone and screamed "I'M NOT A DAD!" and then bought the entire bar a round

Mom: Excuse me? Joe your boyfriend?

Me: Awkward. Ignore that last text.

Dad: and now there are teeth marks on my dick.

Me: Dad that sucks...

Dad: What are you talking about?

Me: Read your last text to me...

Dad: SHIT.

MARIO KART

Me: Jen went down on tom while he played a video game.

Dad: EXCUSE ME WHAT?

Me: Sorry dad that text wasn't for you.

Dad: Was it Mario Kart? That would be the Nintendo Equivalent to road head.

AUTHOR NOTE:
Another personal favorite! Not at all the expected return text, and we'll never look at Mario Kart the same way.

SNOOZE BUTTON

Mom: OMG Jessie, Never following your advice again. So I just tried to wake him up with a blow job and he literally touched the top of my head and said snooze button.

Me: This is your daughter. That is sick.

Mom: What is wrong with trying to spice things up in the bedroom with your father?

Me: This is your daughter.

HAPPIEST DAY OF MY LIFE

Dad: I got used. This is the happiest day of my life. I was just a huge cock and that is all she needed.

Me: DAD WTF?

Dad: Meant to text that to my buddy.

BLACKED OUT

Mom: Blacked out at the beach and unblacked out at a piano bar singing Tiny Dancer.

Mom: Sorry I was drunk last night.

HE WILL ALWAYS BE

Mom: he will always be the guy I fucked in the hallway.

Me: WHO???

REALITY

Dad: drugs are my only escape from this reality. Good thing I got it at a discount price last night

Me: OMG Dad!?!?! I knew it.

Dad: Do as I say not as I do ;)

SOLE PURPOSE IN LIFE

Mom: Sometimes I think my sole purpose in life is to cockblock my Daughter.

Me: Bitch

Mom: ...What it is true.

THAT DISEASE

FROM DAD:

I think I have that disease where you wake up in strange places drunk.

AUTHOR NOTE:
Hmm. Sounds a bit like alcoholism...

LESS CLEAN UP

FROM MOM:

We should start having sex in the shower. Less clean up.

RACK OF RIBS

FROM DAD:

u sent me just one boob. one just doesnt do it for me. u dont get full on a half a rack of ribs, u need a full rack.

AUTHOR NOTE:
OK, this is just clever metaphor play.
More power to you Mr. X.

FOREPLAY

Mom: What the hell do I have to do to get some foreplay around here? This sucks.

Me: Stop Now. You just texted me, YOUR SON.

VOICE MAIL

Mom: She left me a voicemail too. It's just her moaning her name repeatedly

Me: WHO?

Mom: I thought I was texting your father. ummm it was you.

COUGAR HUNTING

Me: Think I'm gonna go cougar hunting tonight…Any advice?

Mom: DON'T.

Me: Wasn't texting you. Convo over.

WOULD IT BE INAPPROPRIATE?

Dad: would it be inappropriate to describe you with the phrase "bigass titties"?

Me: Yes it would DAD.

Dad: Wait who is this?

Dad: That's what you said about that spiderman stripper, but look how that turned out

Me: Dad did you go to a strip club?

Dad: Of course not sweetie.

A GOOD CAUSE

Me: Thank you for the breast cancer awareness themed circle of death. Had it been any other time I would not have played topless.

Mom: Excuse me?

Me: Awkward. Sorry mom I meant to send that to a friend.

Mom: Its ok honey it was for a good cause!

NUVARING

Dad: Should i be worried, I SWALLOWED my wife's nuva ring last night

Me: Umm sick dad how is that even possible?

Dad: Please forget I ever sent this to you i was trying to text Dr. Roberts

LAND BEFORE TIME DVD

Mom: Pack the video camera and we can make another "film" in the hotel room

Mom: Sorry Hun that was for your Dad

Me: Eww Mom seriously?

Mom: Don't watch Land Before Time DVD while we're gone

AUTHOR NOTE:
Can we say latex gloves, a trash bag full of ALL the movies in the family movie collection, and a bonfire while Mom and Dad are gone? Yes, we think so.

PLEASE

Dad: SEEEEXXX PLEASE

Me: GROSSSSSSS!!!!

AUTHOR NOTE:
An A+ for clarity.

RUG BURNS

Mom: So should we discuss the rug burns on my back or just save that for a separate conversation.

Me: Dear God How about NEVER.

Mom: Woops

phase 3:
teaching life lessons

Now our parents felt guilty. They felt like bad, bad parents who had either corrupted their kids or scarred their kids for life...and they probably had. Nonetheless, the parent-child relationship was closer than ever before, because you knew more about each other. There was a tacit agreement that none of those insexts were to be mentioned again—but on a deeper level each side knew that it was an adult understanding now. Not a parent-child understanding. Our relationship with our parents just achieved a new level of intimacy.

Yet guilty they did feel. So, they did their best to make up for it. They tried to be good, decent parents again and offer advice in their text messages. Some of it was downright bizarre, some of it was amusing, some of it was cute, and some of it was inappropriate. But all of it came across as a little bit crazy and completely hilarious.

This chapter is by no means a parenting guide. But if we do say so ourselves, we definitely learned "something" from all these texts…

HOE?

FROM MOM:

Honey if your a hoe that's fine. You have my blood running through your veins. So if u take after your mom that's OK.

KATY PERRY

Me: I'm road-tripping out west with some friends over winter break

Dad: If I send you to California does that mean you're gonna come back wearing daisy dukes and bikinis on top?

JUST A FAVOR

FROM DAD:

Remember Son, sex is not sex till both people cross the finish line. Until then, it's just a favor.

UNHAPPY PAPPY

Dad: we are looking for dog poop cleaners. pay is bad but keeps momma happy as your reward

Me: maybe

Dad: not the response i was looking for....now you have an unhappy pappy

MARIJUANA MATH

FROM MOM:

Remember this very important thing, when you're high, stop smoking. You wont get higher, you'll just have less weed.

AUTHOR NOTE:
Definitely never got this advice from our parents. Talk about being open and honest with your kids.

LAP DANCE

Me: My statistics teacher is getting fired because he had a seminar on strippers and got a lap dance in front of the dean.

Dad: He should have gotten the lap dance for the dean! What was he thinking? Dumb ass.

Mom: It took him longer to undo my bra than he lasted…

Me: excuse me?

Mom: Shouldn't you be doing school work right now.

ALWAYS A DISCOUNT

Me: I hate going over there to get new tires though, its so expensive

Dad: Just put on a low cut shirt; you have big enough boobs to get a discount

Me: Wow, dad, really?

Dad: I'm just saying, you've got huge boobs

MEETING ELLIE

```
FROM MOM:

Hey honey, loved meeting
Ellie, she was really
sweet but she should
shower more, she smelled
like vagina.
```

CHARLIE SHEEN ADVICE

Me: Anything I should work on for the second half?

Dad: Just be aggressive cause I'm pretty sure I gave you Adonis DNA... let's see that Tiger Blood!

AUTHOR NOTE:
We didn't know Charlie Sheen's kids were fans of the site!

RULES OF FIGHTING

FROM DAD:

Here are our rules about fighting: If you get into one and lose, you are grounded. If you get into one and win, I will take you out for ice cream.

PIECE OF TRASH

FROM MOM:

Yes you can have lunch
with your friends but you
cannot wait for matt! No
daughter of mine is going
to be making out in the
parking lot like a piece
of trash!

NOT A SPORT

Me: I would totally fuck that guy in the cut off shirt over there.

Mom: Do we need to have the talk again? Sex IS NOT a sport!! It made you!

WHY YOU DON'T HAVE A BOYFRIEND

Dad: You need to mop the floor and make sure you get down to wipe up so it doesn't leave marks

Me: I don't like getting on my knees

Dad: That's why you don't have a boyfriend

LYNYRD SKYNYRD CONCERT

Me: Omg! I'm at a Lynyrd Skynyrd concert and people are waving actual lighters in the air!!

Dad: Duh u can't lite a joint with a cell phone

ATTA GIRL

Mom: Hi :)

Me: Im drunk! and its noon :)

Mom: atta girl! have fun! no driving. bring condoms.

PUSHUPS

Mom: I just dont know what I am going to do!

Me: Its ok mom. We will make it through this. You are one of the strongest people I know.

Mom: Thats because I do 49 pushups a day!

TORNADOES

Dad: Heard there are tornado warnings...you ok?

Me: Yeah I'm just in the library studying.

Dad: Ok. Hide amongst the books. Tornadoes never hit books, just trailers.

STREET CORNERS

Me: So, I've just realized that I'm going to need some extra money to pay for tuition. Help?

Mom: Well, there's always the street corner.

Me: I need a serious response, mother...

Mom: ...I was being serious.

AUTHOR NOTE:
She's talking about a gourmet
lemonade stand, right?

SCRUB THEM PITS

Mom: Take a shower in 10 mins k ?

Me: okie dokess

Mom: and SCRUB THEM PITS. U R emanating a horrid stench ur scaring the vampires away and the wolves too.

Me: ...

Mom: you stink.

MIGHT AS WELL JOIN THEM

Me: The Justin Bieber movie was AMAZING!

Mom: You need to hop off his dick... besides you will never be as big of a Bilieber as I am.

Me: Mom, you realize he is like 17 right?

Mom: There in nothing wrong with being a cougar, so many women are these days, might as well join 'em.

YOU CAN'T BE SERIOUS

Me: I just don't know what to do. I mean I can get a date from any guy I want, but once they find out I wont have sex with them they just leave. :(What else do I do?

Mom: The only thing you can do. Lay on your back and spread them gorgeous legs.

Me: You can't be serious.

Mom: :)

GOLFING WITH THE GUYS

Me: Dad did you shit your pants when you went golfing with the guys?

Dad: What happens on the golf course stays on the golf course!

I'VE NEVER HAD SEX

Dad: I found a used condom on the trash in your room.

Me: I've never had sex.

Dad: Well not with that attitude, you should really get some.

RUN FAST

Me: I want to go for a jog.

Mom: In this neighborhood? Can you text 9-1-1?

Me: No why?

Mom: Nothing. Run fast.

CHINESE PROVERB

FROM MOM:

"stop drunk texting
mom. it will end only in
shame"--sun tzu

IMPRESS THEM

FROM DAD:

If the cops are flashing
their lights at you, they
just want to see how fast
you can really drive.
Impress them.

AIM BIG

Mom: oh my— i believe your dad is flirting w/ a meth addict right now... oh dear.

Me: um...what.

Mom: daria, all i have to say is...don't settle......aim big.

AUTHOR NOTE:
Brutal honesty, gotta love it.

SHARING

Me: Bus Drama. Driver smelled weed and is threatening to take us back to school.

Mom: Does someone have pot?

Me: Probably, it's high school.

Mom: Well just tell them to share and maybe the bus driver won't take the bus back.

Mom: im just sayin explore your options but explore quickly cause time is of the essence. i feel like wise dahli lama or something.

Me: you are so wise mother.

Mom: just call me dahli mama

HOW TO USE YOUR BIG PURSE

Mom: Do you have any liquor in your purse? You know, like the little bottles they give you on airplanes.

Me: no, why

Mom: This funeral is boring. I need a drink.

Me: I can't believe you just asked me that!

Mom: Well, your purse is big enough to hold some. You should think of putting a flask in there for times like this.

BE SOCIAL

```
FROM DAD:

tell your brother to stop
watching porn and come
be social, there are real
hot girls at this bar.
```

PUNCH BOWLS

Me: I finished my paper so im going to a party tonight!

Dad: Okay watch out for open punch bowls.

Me: we don't drink from punch bowls dad

ORDERING FROM THE MENU

Me: He's looking so hot right now... too bad I have a boyfriend!

Mom: When you're in a relationship, you can look at the menu, you just can't order anything off of it. Sometimes I look at the menu myself.

HOW TO HAVE FRIENDS

Me: Ugh why don't I have friends. people are stupid.....

Dad: When I was your age I started smoking pot and drinking. I had friends

NO BUSCH NO RIDE

Me: Dad i'm really sorry, but i need you to come get me I've been drinking

Dad: Just tell me one thing, was it a Anheuser-busch product?

Me: No

Dad: Find your own way home

MOM'S SIXTH SENSE

DON'T BE A HERO

Dad: Are you leaving work soon? The rain is getting bad.

Me: No, I have to stay.

Dad: well if it gets worse, flee. Don't be a hero

SNOW PLOW

Me: How big is the snow plow's truck? There's a shit ton of snow here

Dad: Generally, you want whoever's plowing you to have a big truck

HITCHHIKING

Me: Can you give me a ride or should I just hitchhike?

Mom: Hitchhike. It's a good way to make friends! Maybe meet Mr. Right!

SAVE A FORTUNE

FROM DAD:

you've had enough chocolate! If you just went out and had some sex you would save a fortune!

IF YOU'RE GOING TO EXPERIMENT IN COLLEGE

Dad: If you're going to experiment in college like I did, use acid or any other liquid drug.

Me: Wait What? Why?

Dad: With your Asthma, you'd take one drag from a joint and your lungs would close up tighter than your mom's hoo-hoo before we had you.

JOB

Me: I was offered a job!

Dad: Accept it before they discover their mistake.

AUTHOR NOTE:
Definitely something our dad would text us.

I WANT YOU TO KNOW

FROM MOM:

Im not trying to scare you away from being gay and all, but I want you to know- anal sex REALLY hurts :(

Me: I can't go to bed now. Pulling an all-nighter for the Bio exam

Mom: You shuld just put the book under ur pillow.

Me: What?

Mom: Then tell ur teacher that osmosis doesnt work and you cant trust his books or his grading.

Send

JEWELRY FROM TIFFANY

FROM MOM:

I'd never kiss a guy if
he got me something from
Kay. But jewelry from
Tiffany, blow job fo sho.

KILLER'S DNA

FROM MOM:

Stop clipping your nails
short! How else are they
supposed to find your
killer's DNA if you are
murdered?

DR. PEPPER

FROM DAD:

Dr. Pepper is obviously good for you. It's not called DOCTOR Pepper for nothing.

DINNER WITH THE FAMILY

Mom: Are you coming home for dinner tonight?

Me: IDK what are you making?

Mom: Oh just put down the joint and come eat dinner with your family.

FINAL EXAM

Me: I failed my last exam :(

Dad: Make your professor give you an A

Me: How?

Dad: Inception

TOO WHITE

Me: I'm trying to tan but there's vultures circling over my head and it's creepy...

Dad: Well maybe it's cause you're so white that they just think your dead.

THEY'LL LEAVE YOU ALONE

FROM MOM:

Honey If your being kidnapped, just poop your pants, They'll leave you alone.

NEVER TRUST...

FROM DAD:

Never trust a priest with a boner. And definitely never trust a nun with a boner.

TELL THEM YOUR PARENTS ARE BITCHES

Me: But all of my friends are going! What will I tell them?

Dad: Well tell them that your parents are bitches.

BUCKET OF GLITTER

FROM DAD:

Son, I know you can't find a girl so I'm gonna offer you some advice... dump a bucket of glitter on yourself and walk into the sunlight. They will come running.

WHAT THEY WANT!

FROM DAD:

Have I given you the talk about what guys want at this age? PORN PORN PORN PORN PORN. And bacon.

CALL GIRL

FROM MOM:

You should be a high class call girl instead of giving it away for free all the time.

BLUE

Me: Everything is better blue.

Dad: Except Balls!

TREASURE HUNT

FROM MOM:

Don't think of it as cleaning your room, think of it as a treasure hunt and the prize is finding the carpet!

TIP OF THE DAY

Me: What do you think of Susan?

Dad: I wouldn't even poke her on facebook.

MOUTH FULL

Me: I really like this girl…but her boobs are really small

Dad: All you really need is a mouth full.

THE PERFECT WORD

FROM DAD:

Boob is the perfect word. The B looks like an aerial view of them, the 2 o's look like a front view and the b looks like a side view.

BUD LIGHT

Dad: I'm disappointed in you

Me: What'd I do?

Dad: I saw those pictures of you on Facebook. I thought I raised you better than to drink Bud Light.

WHEN I WAS A KID

FROM DAD:

When I was a kid, If I didn't wake up with a hard on at Christmas, I didn't have anything to play with

ENTERTAINMENT BUDGET

Me: Mom...I think Im going to start the pill.

Mom: Ok but that'll have to come out of your entertainment budget.

MAKING FACES

FROM DAD:

When a kid makes faces at you through his bus window, follow him home and make faces at him from his bedroom window at night.

HARRY POTTER MATH

FROM DAD:

Let's do some math! Harry Potter > Voldemort. Voldemort > Cedric Diggory. Cedric Diggory = Edward Cullen. Therefore, Harry Potter > Edward Cullen.

SUPPORT GROUP

Me: I hate my job :(

Mom: You know, there's a support group for that. It's called EVERYBODY, and they meet at the bar.

GET A BAG

FROM MOM:

The next time you decide to shave your pubes, make sure you get a bag for the 10 lbs of hair you leave in my razor...

BANK MANAGEMENT

Me: Bad Day?

Mom: Every day I regret the life decisions that led me to bank management and NOT being a coke addicted stripper. Every. Single. Day.

SNOOZE ALARM

> FROM DAD:
>
> I hit the snooze alarm to get a little extra sleep. Instead, I spent the whole time dreading the moment the alarm would go off again.

THEY'RE MY TRICKS!

Dad: Where are you?

Me: On my way home

Dad: Don't lie. You have too much of me in you, I know all your tricks!

BJ'S

Mom: Honey have you ever given a blowjob?

Me: Mom WTF???

Mom: What's the big deal…it's like sucking your thumb. only its not yours and its a penis.

PINOCCHIO'S NOSE

FROM MOM:

Just overheard you talking to that girl, And just want to let you know your penis is not like Pinocchio's nose - it doesn't get longer every time you lie about its size.

HIP PROBLEMS

Me: I'm starting to have hip problems...

Mom: Maybe you should stop spreading your legs so often.

TAUGHT YOU WELL

Mom: So your on birth control, you drink, you smoke cigarettes?

Me: Yes?

Mom: I've never been prouder to call you my daughter

phase 4:
did you *really* just text me that?!

After atoning for their sins, our parents fell into a legitimate comfort level with texting; the no space texts, insexts, and preaching texts had started to subside, and we started chatting like, well, almost like friends. We began using the phone with our parents just like we do with our own peers. They started texting jokes, random bits of information, updates, and pretty much anything else that came across their minds.

At this point, we were thinking to ourselves, "OK, this is kind of neat. I feel normal with my parents now, and I'm comfortable having text conversations with them. I like this." However, we soon came to realize that we didn't know our parents as friends yet. We didn't know how perverted our dad was or how strange our mom could be. They thought that we would be interested in *everything* that they had to say.

We weren't.

For instance, when you were sitting down to watch the football game with your friends, shopping with your girlfriends, or God forbid making out with your significant other, you would get a text from your mom: "Hey! So I just realized why that spot on the couch is your favorite. You were conceived there!" Great. Did you *really* just text your child that, Mom? And did I *really* need to know that? Right now? Well apparently we did.

In Phase 4, our parents comfort level overcame their filter, and they just enjoyed being able to freely text with reckless abandon—about sex, drinking, inappropriate jokes—just like we were friends. The lack of filter provided for some pretty crazy messages, and we showcased what we thought were the funniest ones yet. Enjoy!

Dad

I sent a gift subscription of five gay porn magazines to your moms new boyfriend.

WHY???

I found out they were moving In together and she always wants to be the one to check the mail.

AUTHOR NOTE:
Not gonna lie. After reading this text, we've now thought about doing this to some ex-girlfriends.

TOILET PAPER

Mom: Hey

Me: Why are you texting me, we're in the same house?

Mom: I need you to bring me some toilet paper.

Me: Ew, text dad…

Mom: Nvm, problem solved, but we're going to need a new bathmat.

MARCH MADNESS

FROM DAD:

Kentucky wins!!! They make bourbon there!!!

VICTOR'S SECRET

Dad: I'M GOING IN!!! (sent with a picture of a Victoria Secret store)

Me: OMG...why???

Dad: Idk...maybe a camo thong

MILLIONAIRE MURDER?

Me: Someone won the lottery and they haven't claimed it yet. What is wrong with this person?

Mom: Maybe they are murders and don't want their whereabouts known.

HORNY HONKS

Me: Omg, my horn is going off like crazy. I honked at one person 26 times this morning!!!

Dad: Haha, hope they didn't have a "HONK IF HORNY" bumper sticker ;)

WINE TASTING

Me: Dad! Im going wine tasting

Dad: Swallow don't spit

MOTHERLY LOVE

Mom: I love you honey!

Me: Awe I love you too Mom. :-)

Mom: No...seriously I'm grateful for you. Cause when I look at others people's kids they are just retarded morons.

HALF AN HOUR

FROM DAD:

Just spent half an hour
trying to take your mom's
bra off, I wish I'd never
tried it on!

MAKING COOKIES

Me: Okay, we're at Johns, making cookies.

Dad: K as long as its not babies.

CAR SEAT

Mom: I just watched a show that said based on your height u should still b in a car seat lol

Me: Mom im 19

RETURNING THE FAVOR

Me: Why are you trying to ruin my life??

Mom: Just returning the favor hunny.

Me: What? I never ruined your life!

Mom: No, but you did ruin my vagina.

BORROW MINE!

Mom: What are you doing?

Me: My friends are looking at vibrators online.

Mom: Don't bother buying any—Just use mine!

REMOTE'S BROKEN

Mom: The remotes broken and I'm stuck watching porn.

Me: Why would you tell me that?

Mom: Incase you and your friends come in and I'm still watching it.

DISNEY LAND

FROM DAD:

It's like a big Disney Land where you can drink while picking up a hooker on the corner. Heading out sightseeing! Love you

BAD DREAM

Mom: I had a horrible dream about you last night....

Me: What is it? I probably died.

Mom: No, it's worse....you were pregnant...

YOUR MOM'S

Dad: (. .)

Me: did you just send me boobs?

Dad: lol yes

Me: (.) (.) these are perkier

Dad: (ten minutes later) |.| |.| your moms boobs

TEXTING AND DRIVING

Mom: Are you home?

Me: No I'm smoking weed shooting heroine and thinking about contracting a sexually transmitted disease tonight

Mom: Good just hope you are not texting and driving

SEX GPS

AUTHOR NOTE:
A good idea? Yes. Something we want to hear from Mom? No.

GLEEKING OUT

> FROM DAD:
>
> Come into the kitchen, I'm gleeking it out in here.

FACEBOOK ADDICT

Me: Hey mom, you still awake?

Mom: Yep. Doing my cityville on facebook. What do you want? I don't have time to talk...I have crops to harvest, businesses to run, and no damn energy left!

IN LIGHT OF SAINT PATTY'S DAY

Mom: Who's Irish and has to live outside?

Me: Who?

Mom: Patty O'Furniture!

SWEET 16

Me: What are you getting me for my 16th birthday?

Mom: Your virginty back. I know all about your antics at 15 young lady. Don't think I'm stupid.

Me: Sorry?

Mom: Just don't get pregnant. I'm to much of a MILF to be a GILF.

NUTSACK

Dad: Last time I saw the bears win the super bowl, you were still swimming in my nutsack

Me:...wow

CIRCUMCISED

Mom: I just want you too know that we got you circumcised

Me: yes i noticed mom

Mom: tell your girlfriend i say your welcome

WAIT A MINUTE

Dad: Hey Honey did you pick up those asshole yet?

Me: I didn't know I was supposed to and I don't have a car.

Dad: Shit I meant to send this to your mom.

Me: Wait assholes?....Are you talking about me and Robbie?

SECURITY BREACH

Dad: Good morning are you looking forward to being groped by the TSA?

Me: Thanks for that, dad.

Dad: Don't wear panties and see if they can tell.

POSSE

Me: sorry i didn't answer your call, i was at a bookstore

Dad: its saturday night! why arent you rounding up a posse of conservatives and throwing rocks at liberals?

BOOTY DUTY

Me: Dad, the dress costs $800.

Dad: WHAT!! Do you know how much booty duty im going to have to do around the corner now?

SHAMPOO

Mom: Now I know why I'm fat!

Me: why?

Mom: The shampoo I use says "Adds body and volume" I should shower with dishwashing soap that says "removes even the toughest grease"

SHOTGUN

PREGNANT

Mom: Hey honey, how r u?

Me: Hey mom, im good, wbu?

Mom: well i need to tell u something...Im pregnant...

Me: mom, i am too...

Mom: omg! i was joking!!

Me: oh...

STRIP POKER?

Mom: what are you guys doing?

Me: playing apples to apples.

Mom: as long as it's not strip poker.

AUTHOR NOTE:
Who said it wasn't Strip Apples to Apples?

ORAL SEX TIPS

Mom: Honey, do you have any oral sex tips?

Me: um, no. awk

Mom: Should i just suck it like u do to ur camelbak?

Me: Seriously MOM STOP

HE'S SEEN *THE HANGOVER* TOO MANY TIMES

Me: I am at church. Where are you?

Dad: We are in Vegas...there is a tiger in the bathroom. Can't make it to church.

BIRTH CONTROL

FROM DAD:

hi havent talked to you in awhile do you need birth control?

BOMB THREAT

Me: bomb threat at school.

Dad: don't get blown up or your grounded

SOY MILK

FROM DAD:

Does soy milk mean I am milk in Spanish?

I'M NOT A WHORE, MOM

Me: I am bring my friend Ron back to watch a movie

Mom: Ok, Make sure you use a condom

Me: wtf we are watching a movie I am not a whore mom

FUNKY JUNK

Mom: Condoms condoms condoms!

Me: Never!!!

Mom: Ok but don't come crying to me when you get funky junk.

PORN STASH

Mom: I'm sad.

Me: Why?

Mom: Your dad's sexual life is better then mine.

Me: Does this mean he is cheating?

Mom: No. It means he found your porn stash!

SPERM ODOR

Mom: I know when and where you wank.

Me: MOM! WTF!

Mom: Yes, you've got the same sperm-odor as your father. So when you wank I detect it.

Me: End of this conversation.

AUTHOR NOTE:
We agree. Although we would have added, "Don't ever text me again."

HAVE FUN TONIGHT

Mom: Have you left yet?

Me: Yeah, I'm on my way now.

Mom: OK. Have fun tonight...I hope no one sees your vagina (;

MAGICIAN

Dad: Im calling the Maury Show because Im not sure Mom is your real mother

Me: um...weren't you there when i like...popped out?

Dad: THAT PROVES NOTHING! think about it! you and i are so smart and got our shit together. she could have hired a magician like criss angel or david copperfield to trick us!

DAD WATCHES THE GRAMMYS

FROM DAD:

Justin Bieber is on now.
He is steamy

YOU GET WHAT YOU WISH FOR

FROM DAD:

when i was 17 i said i
wanted to be like heff
and be surrounded by
women...i didnt mean
a wife, ex-wife, and 5
daughters

WEINER CALLED

FROM MOM:

Omg. Les wiener just called me and I can't stop laughing. Rather have more wiener call me!

TAX RETURN

Dad: you got a 108$ tax return

Me: yay, I need money, can you send it to me?

Dad: Slow down Paris Hilton, I'll give it to you if you survive the rapture. Cant waste money these days.

SERIOUSLY

FROM MOM:

I just pooped so big it looped around into a knot

STINKY HAND HERP

Me: Punch her in the vag!

Mom: I wouldn't cuz my hand would stink and go in to far. I dont want to get the hand herp!

Mom: No stinky hand herp here!

AUTHOR NOTE:
Now that is one hell of a good
mother-daughter relationship.

DON'T GET BANGED

Me: hey im going out for the night.

Dad: ok sweet heart dont get gang banged.

Me: -_____-

NO BUTT SEX

Me: Is it all right if I stay at my friends house?

Dad: I don't care

Dad: But no butt sex!

HIP MOM QUOTES 50 CENT

FROM MOM:

I miss you like a fat kid misses cake!

DA BIZ

Me: Oliver Stone is coming to our school on Thursday for a Q&A

Dad: I'm curious to see what he's like. A lot of varying opinions in da biz.

BEST BREASTS ON CAMPUS

Dad: On Direct TV They have Girls Gone Wild-Best Breasts on Campus. I'm looking for y'all and Toledo students.

Me: Gross Dad your looking for your daughters boobs on TV

HAMSTERS

FROM MOM:

sometimes i wish we
were hamsters. they eat
their young when they
misbehave.

FEELING GOOD

FROM MOM:

I loved being pregnant
with you! I felt great
the whole time! I haven't
felt good since, but
that's not the point.

HIP GRANDMA

Me: How is the trip so far?

Grandma: We are in a limo heading to the hotel, cause that's how Dirty D and Papa B roll!

STONED OFF YOUR ASS

FROM DAD:

(1:44 am) If someone threw a rock and knocked you off your donkey.... does that make you stoned off your ass?

TEXT A HO

Mom: When the weather outside is frightful, and hot sex sounds so delightful, and when there's no one else you know, txt a ho txt a ho txt a ho.

Me: MOM!

Mom: What? Your uncle sent it to me.

I'LL LET HIM KNOW

Me: I don't know how to tell you this but is there anyway you can be a little more quieter at night. I can't study. ewwww

Mom: That wasn't me that was your dad but I'll let him know.

RIDE 'EM

Me: we're doing the whole exam; stirrups and everything. oh and i'm also getting on birth control.

Mom: ok, ride 'em cowgirl!

Me: i'm pretending you didn't say that.

I DON'T GO AWAY

Mom: What are the chances of you going to the Dentists next week?

Mom: DON'T IGNORE ME. I'M LIKE HERPES, I DON'T GO AWAY!

I DON'T HAVE AN STD

Me: I have a very important question for you!!!

Dad: The answer is doxycycline three times a day for seven days. Haha!

STILL A MAN

Dad: When u and ur bf have sex do u give or receive?

Me: Wow, um, I'm not even going to honor that question with a response.

Dad: What?! I just want to know if my son is still kind of a man.

AUTHOR NOTE:
I can't tell if this dad is being supportive or not. Oh well, let's give him the benefit of the doubt.

DR. EVIL

Me: how much does it cost to rent a movie

Dad: one miiiilllliiiiiiiiiiioooooonn dollars

TACO BELL

Dad: What did you get at Taco Bell?

Me: Food

Dad: Shut the fuck up

HOW'S IT HANGIN'?

Me: hey mom, how's it hangin'?

Mom: low :P

Me: huh?

Mom: babe I'm bra shopping leave me alone.

UNFRIENDED

FROM MOM:

I'm sorry you guys broke up. I unfriended him on Facebook.

Mom

I wonder what teachers do when we have a day off from and they don't???

I would assume they get drunk and run through the hallways naked.

ANYTHING HEAVY

Me: What did the doc say?

Dad: Not supposed to lift anything heavy so i have to start sitting down when I pee.

COCKTAIL PARTY

FROM DAD:

What makes a good cocktail party? A lot of cock and a whole lot of tail.

WASTE OF TIME

Dad: Do they fuck in the end of "Lady and the Tramp" or am I just wasting my time?

Me: Dad WTF? It's a Disney Movie

Dad:...So a waste of time?

FAIR WARNING

FROM DAD:

You better come get your gf. White pants, black thong. Mom's jealous and somehow I'm in trouble. you know which direction this shit storm is rolling.

TABOO WITH FRIENDS

Me: Im playing Taboo with friends. Our last one was "something you do on your knees"

Mom: Oh I know! Blow Job! BLOW JOB!

Me: No Mom! It's Pray

PITCH OF JUSTIN BIEBER

FROM DAD:

Just sucked the helium out of a balloon, and tried singing, I finally matched the pitch of Justin Bieber.

UNCOMFORTABLE

Mom: I wanted to give your bf a hug!

Me: Why didn't you?

Mom: I'm not wearing a bra and it would probably make him feel uncomfortable.

LADY WIPES

Dad: How was work last night?

Me: Awful, I hate catering jobs... I came home smelling like a shrimp cocktail

Dad: Well your definitely your mothers daughter I will tell her to send you some of those special lady wipes she uses they really help

Me: SICK

JUSTICE WILL BE SERVED

Mom

Me: Send more cookies my roommate ate all of them before I got one.

Mom: I will send another batch but make sure not to eat any I am going to teach him a lesson.

Me: Oh no. What are you going to do?

Mom: Laxatives! Justice will be served.

MAYBE

FROM MOM:

Maybe it's about time
your left leg should meet
your right leg.!

SHE GOT IT FROM HER DADDY

FROM MOM:

You and your sister
inherited your big boobs
from your father.

HOGWARTS ROBE

Me: Hey Dad can you call me when you get this!

Dad: Nope, too busy pretending that my snuggie is a Hogwarts robe.

RED PANTS

FROM DAD:

I would have more money
if I didn't have to buy
your stupid pads. Can't
you wear red pants so
nobody can tell?

TROLL DAD AT IT AGAIN...
FO DRIZZLE

Dad: Hey! Why does Snoop Dog carry an umbrella?

Me: Umm idk?

Dad: Fo DRIZZLE

COLD WEATHER

Me: I hate it here it is so cold :(

Dad: I love cold weather!

Me: what is wrong with you?

Dad: Cold weather makes me feel like a dragon when I breathe.

KNEE-JERK REACTION

Dad: Will you marry me?

Me: EW NO! DAD!

Dad: Good. We'll just keep practicing this so that when someone actually asks you to marry them it'll just be a knee-jerk reaction.

SWALLOW WHO??????

FROM MOM:

Sometimes you make me so angry, I wish I had swallowed you!!!!

A BETTER WORLD

FROM DAD:

I dream of a better world...a world where a chicken can cross the road without his motives being questioned

BARN DOOR

Me: Your barn door is open.

Dad: It doesn't matter when your horse is dead

RASPBERRY TEA

Dad: I took your suggestion and got the raspberry tea from Sonic

Me: And how did you like it?

Dad: It tastes like licking a stripper!

A TATTOO

Me: Mom I'm gonna get a tattoo.

Mom: The only tattoo I'll allow you to get is eyeballs on the bottom of ur boobs so when you get old and saggy you can fling em over your shoulder and scare the crap outta the neighbor kids

GOOGLE EARTH

Me: Hey what are you up to?

Dad: I'm looking at pot farms on google earth.

COURT ROOMS

FROM DAD:

I don't believe these are real court rooms. They look absolutely nothing like law and order.

TIME SPACE CONTINUUM

Me: Goodnight Daddy!

Dad: Within the time space continuum of alternating states of mind and soul I hope you have a pleasant and non refractory interim before somnolence.

REPLACEMENT

Mom: ...And after we had to put Buddy down, I decided that I wanted something that would outlive me so I had you.

Me: So I'm a replacement for a cat?

Mom: Yep. Love you, Honey

I HEARD A THUD

Me: Dad are you OK I heard a thud from upstairs

Dad: Yeah just dropped my penis

LIKE A BOSS

FROM DAD:

I just farted in the dogs face to show him who's boss

CONTACT LIST

Me: Hey

Dad: Who is this...I have all my childrens names changed to asshole. Which one are you?

BIG NEWS!!!

FROM DAD:

BIG NEWS!!! The National Mustard Museum in town was vandalized. With ketchup.

BEST MONDAY EVER

FROM DAD:

Got to see someone fall down the stairs while holding hot coffee and a folder full of papers. Best Monday ever.

THE HOBO

Me: Dad, who do I look like more, you or Mom?

Dad: You look like the hobo who gave you to us.

THEY REALLY EXIST!

Dad: Porn bloobers exist! never have I laughed so hard while jerking off!

Me: WTF is wrong with you. Don't ever text me agian.

Dad: We are all adults here.

HOW ABOUT?

Me: How about we go see Inception

Dad: I'm sorry i'm just too high to handle anything besides pirates of the Caribbean right now.

CUPCAKE

FROM MOM:

Putting a pretty shirt over your muffin top does not make you a cupcake.

THAT RACK

Me: I'M 23 I am tired of people thinking I'm still 15!

Dad: With THAT rack?

YOU DESERVE...

FROM MOM:

You deserve a hand job from Edward scissor hands.

WAFFLE STAGE

Me: Hey Dad! What are you up to?

Dad: I am currently in the waffle making stage of highness

BUMPIT

FROM DAD:

I bet I could wear a Bumpit under my mustache.

YOUR FRIEND'S MOM

Dad: It just hit me that I made out with your friend's mom last night... I think it was John's mom.

Me: WTF. As in John my boyfriend?

Dad: Error your text has not been received.

Me: DAD???? I can't believe you.

OMG I FOUND HIM!!!

FROM MOM:

I found Waldo on Twitter and I now follow him. I feel accomplished bc not only have I found him, but I can follow him and know where he is at all times.

A DESERT SHE WILL NEVER FORGET...

Dad: Honey could you pick a few things up for your mother and I at the store on your way home?

Me: Sure what do yall need

Dad: hershey syryp, redi-whip, cherries and glow stix... Im going to make her a desert she will never forget... Me :)

Me: Gross i dont even want to know what the glow sticks are for

ANDY'S MOM'S TOYS

FROM DAD:

I wonder if Buzz and Woody ever met any of Andys moms toys. Especially since they probably have the same names...

➡ phase 5:
dad for the win

Slowly, we reached a point where the random bits of information and "trivia" were too much. So we just stopped responding. Then, like us when we were teenagers, our parents became resentful of our lack of communication. They didn't hate us like we hated them when we were high school, but they sure texted like it sometimes.

You see, our parents started feeling like we had gotten too comfortable with them now. They had to reassert their dominance.

Mom came later, because let's face it, she's nicer. But Dad? He went straight for the kill. He thought: "Oh, so you'll be selective about when you respond to me? Is that right? Well bring it on, son. You just entered into a world of pain, because

when I do get to hear from you now, you're going to regret it."
In a good natured kind of way though, of course.

And enter a world of pain we did. We were forced to respect our father's ability to completely own us. We thought we were good at belittling people and burning them pretty hard, but Dad really went for the win—and he'd had twenty or so odd years of experience doing so before we came along.

Needless to say he won. He won with style, too; his crazy texts forced us to respect his charm, wit, and dominance. Who ever would have thought?

EQUAL OPPORTUNITY

Dad: You know I'm an equal opportunity hater

Me: I know, but you love me :D

Dad: Your mother says I have to

BABY, BABY, BABY, OHHHHH

Me: Dad, i am not a baby no more

Dad: Yes you are my little Justin Bieber "Baby, Baby, Baby, ohhhhh"

GETTING IN SHAPE

Me: I need to get in shape

Dad: Round is a shape, kind of

AUTHOR NOTE:
Can't argue with pure logic.

MAGNIFYING GLASS

Dad: Have you ever bought anything on eBay?

Me: Yeah why?

Dad: I think I just wasted some money on eBay, I bought a penis enlargement kit and the dude sent me a magnifying glass.

PENCIL ME IN

Me: Can you come get me around seven?

Dad: Maybe

Me: well, lemme know when you can pencil it into your busy schedule of bejeweled and checking your email, ok?

Dad: haha ur funny. Pencil me in for never.

NO PUN INTENDED

Dad: Were you finally able to poop?

Me: Nope.

Dad: well shit

Dad: No pun intended

CAN'T FIND IT?

Me: I'm going to get a tattoo of either a banana or a hot dog on my upper leg

Dad: Son, Are you trying to tell me you can't find it?

STOP TWEETING

Me: Whens my iPad sposed to come?

Dad: As soon as u stop tweeting 100 times a day

10%

Me: I got a 90% on my calc test!

Dad: What happened to the other 10%?

TRANSITIONS GLASSES

Dad: Shut up! I cant stand you and your transsexual glasses!

Me: Dad, they're called TRANSITIONS.

Dad: Whatever. They still make you look like a lesbian.

5 FISHEEZ 4 U

Me: Please please please PLEASE don't make me go on that fishing trip. I promise I'll clean the house, I won't talk back, and I'll be a good child for the rest of my life.

Dad: ><\\\o>. ><\\\o>. ><\\\o>. ><\\\o>. ><\\\o>. 5 fisheez 4 u

A LITTLE SYMPATHY

Me: Geez Dad, it's been a bad day, can I just get a little sympathy?

Dad: You want sympathy? Look it up in the dictionary its between shit and syphilis.

EAT ME!

Dad: Your an ass...

Me: Your a Vagina

Dad: Well you know what? EAT ME!

A WHAT?

Me: Dad, what do I do if a condom breaks?

Dad: A what?

PISSED OFF

Me: I can't handle these people anymore. Everyone pisses me off.

Dad: It's better to be pissed off than pissed on.

DISNEY LAND

Dad: Why did Snow White get kicked out of Disney Land =)?

Me: ummm why dad?

Dad: She sat on Pinocchio's face and said lie to me

LOSING WEIGHT

Me: I'm losing weight!!!

Dad: TURN AROUND AND YOU'LL FIND IT!

RESIGNED

Me: Hahah that Weiner guy resigned

Dad: I guess he finally realized it was time to Pull Out

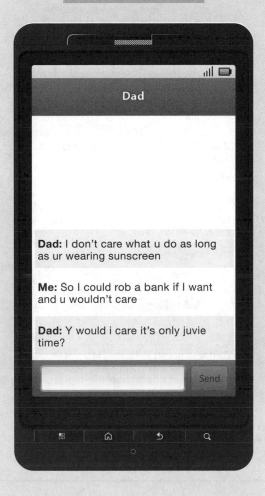

Dad: I don't care what u do as long as ur wearing sunscreen

Me: So I could rob a bank if I want and u wouldn't care

Dad: Y would i care it's only juvie time?

DON'T DO ANYTHING I WOULDN'T

Me: I'm going to a party tonight. That ok?

Dad: Ok, don't do anything I wouldn't

Me: That leaves a lot to do, then have sex, drugs, alcohol…

Dad: you can't get pregnant because I didn't

TOPLESS POOL

Dad: I'm bored in Miami. Mom is in Tampa all day and I'm stuck by myself at the topless hotel pool looking at boobies.

Me: And thats boring why???

Dad: Only the men are topless.

BOARDING SCHOOL

Me: Did you and mom read me Madeline to prepare me for being shipped off to boarding school?

Dad: that was the idea.

Me: what happened?

Dad: no one would accept you.

PEOPLE SUCK

Me: Well people suck.

Dad: Wish more females did. Let me know if you have too man

A SENIOR

Me: I'm a senior!

Dad: Congratulations, so am I.

YOUR ROOMMATE

Dad: Your roommate sounds like a party girl.

Me: She drinks, doesn't smoke though.

Dad: She would smoke if she caught on fire.

PEOPLE IN HELL

Me: Jordi wanted me to tell you he wants pizza

Dad: people in hell want ice water too.

WHEN YOU HAVE KIDS...

Me: I can't wait to have kids one day, so I can make them do all of the house work.

Dad: I can't wait either. That way, you will see what kind of fucked up shit I put up with on a daily basis. ALL of the housework? Dusting and vacuuming ONE day this year does not constitute ALL of the housework.

WOW THANKS

Me: Dad, am i a bastard?

Dad: No your just a bitch.

Me: wow thanks.

AUTHOR NOTE:
Always look for the silver lining. He did say "just."

DRUG TEST

Me: Everything is a go at my new job, I just have to pass the drug test in the morning.

Dad: You better study really fuckin' hard for that.

Dad: Do you need any of that fake pee stuff?

JOKE'S ON YOU SON

Me: Jokes on you I keep submitting ur texts to "crazy things parents text"

Dad: I write your phone number on bathroom walls

WHAT ARE YOU UP TO?

Me: Hey Dad, what are you up to?

Dad: About 5'9"

EXTRA WEIGHT

Me: Just landed!

Dad: Did the plane have trouble taking off with all the weight your mom put on?

SOMETHING SMALL

Dad: R u getting ur brother a bday pres

Me: Yeah I was going to with something small

Dad: U mean like a condom

Me: We're in the auditorium getting lectured on sex...

Dad: Are you the guest speaker?

SOMETHING USEFUL

Me: Get off of facebook and do something useful.

Dad: Mom is useful, can I do her?

STICKS AND STONES

Dad: Honey, I love you but you are STUPID.

Me: Sticks and stones can break my bones but words never hurt me.

Dad: Oh yeah, avada kedavra.

HELEN KELLER

Dad: How are finals? Have they started?

Me: Had my capstone and final speech for public speaking last week. Now all I have left is a paper and my nonverbal communication final project/presentation on friday.

Dad: How does a person give a non verbal speech? Do u Helen Keller thru it?

LIKE A TUMOR

Me: Did mom have a c-section with me?

Dad: Yep Thats right. You weren't born you were surgically removed... Like a tumor.

STUPID MISTAKE!

Me: Dad, I think I made a stupid mistake!

Dad: That was the same thing I told your grandfather 9 months before you were born.

KNEES & TOES

Dad: If you need anything text me.

Me: okay

Me: head and shoulders

Dad: KNEES & TOES

WHO IS THIS?

Me: What time are you picking me up?

Dad: Who is this?

Me: Your son.

Dad: How did you get this number?

Me: I programmed your phone, remember?

Dad: How do I delete people?

DON'T EMBARRASS YOUR FAMILY

Me: Aren't you going to tell me to break a leg?

Dad: No However I will tell you don't suck, don't embarrass your family and if you do, don't come home.

SOMETHING STUPID

FROM DAD:

About to do something
stupid. You'll be my
call. Bring bail money.

DAD'S TAKE ON *TWILIGHT* VS. *HARRY POTTER*

FROM DAD:

The fact that Edward
Cullen was originally a
hufflepuff explains so much.

PECKER

Me: Can I borrow 50 dollars I want to buy Carly a present.

Dad: Money's not like your pecker. It wont grow in your hand.

FORTUNE COOKIE

FROM DAD:

I'm on the toliet eating
a fortune cookie and it
said "Force it to be
successful"

LOW BLOW

Dad: You're going to hang out with your friends after your workout?

Me: Yeah, it wasn't that rough of a workout

Dad: So that's why you don't have a boyfriend.

Me: Low blow, dad.

MEMORY

Dad: I think I have a pornographic memory.

Me: Don't you mean photographic?

Dad: No.

CROSS THAT BRIDGE

Me: What are you goin to do when Eliza turns 16 and wants to start dating?

Dad: We'll cross that bridge when we throw her off of it.

TWILIGHT MOVIE

Me: Dad have you seen My Twilight movie? I need some Eward Cullen in my life!

Dad: Dear Amanda, Vampires are dead. With no blood it's impossible they'd get an erection. Enjoy fantasizing about that.

MOVIE STAR

Me: If I was in a movie, would you ever watch it?

Dad: I don't watch porn

AUTHOR NOTE:
We could only hope our father had the same high hopes for us.

HOOD OF THE CAR

Me: What kind of animal is on the hood of a Jaguar?

Dad: Why did you have to be born blonde?

GOING TO THE STORE

FROM DAD:

Im going to the store
but unlike your mom I'll
actually come back

GOING SOMEWHERE?

Mom: (Mass text) Did anyone see my broom?

Dad: Why? Are you going somewhere?

RINGTONE

Dad: Just sent you this ringtone. Please make it my personal ringtone on your phone.

Me: Dad this is the Darth Vader Imperial March theme...

DAD THINKS HE'S WITTY...

Me: Hey! I think you just butt called me

Dad: I just wanted to ass you a question!

RETARD

Dad: How is the party?

Me: Lame. Its really gay.

Dad: Gay is not an appropriate term. Retard

CHILDISH

Dad: Okie

Me: Dokie

Dad: Artie

Me: Chokie

Dad: Yeah, that's what your mom did last night!!

WHO OWES MORE?

Me: You owe me $350 for the ipad.

Dad: Ok. You owe me hundreds of thousands for your entire life.

I GOT SKILLS

Dad: Hey

Me: Hey what are you doing?

Dad: Peeing

Me: Dad?!?!

Dad: Thats right I got skills. I can text and pee at the same time.

QUIT SMOKING

Me: If you would quit smoking we wouldn't have this problem.

Dad: If I were a virgin we wouldn't be having this conversation.

DAD TEXTS BOYFRIEND

Dad

Dad: What can you do for my daughter?

BF: I'd die for her!

Dad: I don't like you.

BF: Why?

Dad: Im looking for someone who would just live for her, not someone who would just die and leave her alone.

Send

NAILING IT

Me: Playing the guitar hero game you got me. I love the feeling of nailing a solo.

Dad: I love the feeling of nailing a hot chick.

THE OLD PLACE

Me: The old place looks like a whore house.

Dad: Impossible...You moved out

IT'S SMILING AT ME!

Dad: How do women not know they have a camel toe?

Me: Dad???

Dad: Lady, your vagina is smiling at me!

SURVEILLANCE EXPERT

Dad: You look like a slut in your FB photos. Please take down your album "Summer Lovin"

Me: Stalk much Dad?

Dad: Stalking is such a strong word I prefer the term surveillance expert.

GOATS

Dad: Your pretty hot

Me: You're not supposed to notice that.

Dad: Then how am I supposed to know how many goats I have to throw in when I marry you off?

SLING SHOT

FROM DAD:

Son your date is so ugly, when you bring her over to the house for dinner we will have to tie her in the corner and feed her with a sling shot.

LADY GAGA AND STEAK

EPISODE OF *GLEE*

Dad: Stop singing all the time.

Me: Why?

Dad: Your life is not an episode of fucking Glee

AWKWARD

Me: Dad it was so awkward...

Dad: You know whats awkward is yelling, 'HEY SLUT' and watching 15 girls turn around.

DISOWN

Me: Dad, prepare to disown me.

Dad: DID YOU BUY A JUSTIN BEIBER CD?!

BORED

FROM DAD:

im bored, i think ill put on a grim reaper costume and stand across the street from the nearest nursing home and wave at the old folks...

POKE!

FROM DAD:

I'm searching Facebook for people named Hontas, just because I think it would be cool...to poke a Hontas.

RELATIONSHIP STATUS

Dad: You changed your relationship status to 'It's complicated' on Facebook?

Me: Yeah why?

Dad: Can't decide which hand to use?

27 MARSHMALLOWS

Dad

Me: I just shoved 27 marshmellows in my mouth

Dad: Well thats nice change of pace from what you normally put in your mouth.

Send

GIRL OUT LATE

FROM DAD:

For a girl who's supposed to be a virgin you stay out awfully late.

WINNING

Dad: How much coke did Charlie Sheen take?

Dad: Enough to kill two and a half men

WHAT IF I TOLD YOU...

Me: What would you do if I told you my gf got pregnant?

Dad: I'd say lets go find the guy and kick his ass!

LIKE M&M'S

FROM DAD:

Girls are like M&M's, once the lights go out you can't tell the difference.

JEALOUS

FROM DAD:

Does your ass ever get jealous of the shit that comes out of your mouth?

→ phase 6:
mom for the win

Of course Dad will give you a hard time, that's his job. But your Mom? Never! She loved you, tucked you in at night, read to you, and took care of you when you were sick. This sweet, mild-mannered lady can't have the same unparallelled wit and vitriol that your father possessed, could she?

Damn right she could.

You know *exactly* what we are talking about, too. Were you adopted and didn't know about it? Well, neglect to text your mom in Phase 6, and you'll know. Too busy to text your mom back after a whole day? Guess what, you came out of her damn vagina and she'll let you know that.

Basically there are no lines she won't cross or words she won't say if she doesn't have to look you in the eyes. And she has some crazy-ass stuff to say.

But don't take our word for it, check out to what lengths Mom is willing to go for the win in real life!

CARING MOTHER

Me: Mom I forgot my glasses at home! I can't see the game :(

Mom: Loser

NUDE BEACH

Me: If I go on springbreak I'm goin to need more bathing suits

Mom: Go to a nude beach

OPEN WINDOW

Me: Ugh I'm just going to jump out the window

Mom: Hold on I'll open it for you

ADDED BOOBAGE

Mom: How's my pres of the itty bitty titty committee doing?

Me: I'm a C-cup! And I'm fine.

Mom: You're a B-cup who puts their arm rolls into the bra for added boobage

AMBIEN

Mom: Your father is driving me crazy when are you coming home!!!

Me: Im out with friends so not till late sorry!!

Mom: Its ok I put Ambien in his tea... he wont be annoying me much longer.

NERDS GONE WILD

> **FROM MOM:**
>
> instead of GGW y'all are nerds gone wild...you should go to the library and mix up the books!!

DAD WITH THE LABEL MAKER

> **FROM MOM:**
>
> If you see your dad with the label-maker, take it from him! I keep finding stickers all around the house that say "Doug is cool."

Mom: Where are you? It's past midnight. Respect your curfew

Me: I'm at the store.

Mom: Store? The only thing open past midnight are your legs.

Me: Wow thanks.

AUTHOR NOTE:
No coming back from that one.

TIGER WOODS

Mom: Who are you with?

Me: New guy - You haven't met him yet...

Mom: Tiger Woods don't got shit on you.

BUGGERS!

Me: Yuckie. There's a boy in the bus picking his nose.

Mom: Ask him if its lunch or dessert

A FACT

Me: This harry potter stuff is stupid...

Mom: Here is a FACT, The existence of Hogwarts has never been proven false.

OFFERED A JOB...

Me: I just got offered a job...

Mom: Honey, prostitution is still illegal in Ontario, but at least you were offered.

Me: -_-

PRESENTS

Me: Mom your Facebook says today is your birthday...

Me: It's not your birthday

Mom: I know but all my stupid friends bought me presents, I kind of like it

AUTHOR NOTE:
Like we said earlier, you learn something new every day. Think we might just try this one out.

SUPPORT

Me: Bought sports bras at target and charged to your card...is that ok?

Mom: Yup- I have to support, Support! LOL!

BOWEL MOVEMENT

Me: OK I don't even have enough energy to pass a bowel movement... Isn't that sad?

Mom: are you full of shit?

GETTING FLOWERS

Me: I think I'm getting flowers on my date tonight.

Mom: Did you put out already?

LAME KIDS

Mom: Your father and I are thinking of adopting.

Me: That's nice but you have 3 kids....

Mom: Yeah but we want a chance to have a cool one, and we have given our DNA three tries already. Eh, what can I do, I got lame kids.

SKANK

Mom: All the boys are here watching the game and they said your brother's gf reminds them of you. ewwww.

Me: Gross I'm not a Latina skank.

Mom: Not Latina anyway...

SAVING CALL

Mom: Drive safe! What movie are you seeing? Dad says does Chris know he's gay?

Me: Mom! Lmfao tell Dad Chris is not gay, he's in touch with his feelings.

Mom: Is that a no to the "Come home now Grandma died" call?

MOM NEEDS TOILET PAPER

Mom: hey sweetie I'm on the toilet right now and there is no toilet paper, would you mind getting me a roll?

Me: not really I'm busy watching tv

Mom: okay I'm gonna use your new shirt. Maybe next time you will listen to me and clean up after yourself. Love you <3

Mom

Me: Mom tyler is coming over!

Mom: Whoooo!

Me: ???

Mom: For a second i thought you were lesbian since you haven't brought any guys home in the last 8 months.

Me: thanks mom.

Send

HIDE YO KIDS

FROM MOM:

There has been a rise of burglaries in town, so the alarm is on. They're climbin' in our windows, snatchin' our people up.

A PHONE CALL

Mom: Call me!

Mom: Its me, Call me!

Mom: Call Me ASAP! HELLO?

Mom: I PUSHED YOU OUT OF MY VAGINA BUT YOU'RE TOO DAMN LAZY TO MAKE A PHONE CALL!?!

Mom

I found the essays I wrote when I applied to business schools. I BSed them all.

I found my acceptance letters to BU, Dartmouth, Brown, Columbia, and other schools!

I am so smart! You guys got your dad's genes.

FINGERS CROSSED

Me: I'm keeping my fingers crossed!

Mom: and your legs

Me: For extra luck? Or because you think I'm a slut?

Mom: I've seen your facebook posts...

YOU CAN'T FOOL MOM

Mom: Stop masturbating it's time for dinner.

Me: I'm watching a movie...

Mom: Just come to dinner.

Mom: And wash your hands!

BAG OF POT

Me: Mom, can I have $20 so I can go to the movies?

Mom: Wow, a bag of pot was only $5 when I was a kid!

CONTRACEPTIVES

Me: What did you buy at the drug store?

Mom: Contraceptives. I didn't get you any. Because You don't get any…

Me: …

YOU GET IT FROM YOUR MOMMA

FROM MOM:

You get it from your momma. Just kidding sweetie, you really don't. At least I have boobs enough for the both of us. Love you!

MS. SLUTTTTS-O-LOT

Me: okay well then can I hang out with James or Chris? I don't wanna hang out with Chase, maybe i can hang out with Robert? is that okay??

Mom: you are such a little slut.

Me: mom were all just friends

Mom: whatever you say ms.slutttts-o-lot

Me: Sorry I didn't see you there

Mom: Yes you did. Stop pretending!

Me: I'm not!

Mom: Yeah well next time I'll pretend i don't see you in front of the car when I'm driving

IRISH PUB

Mom: how did you spend $83 at tommy condoms?

Me: haha, condon's not condoms ma, it's an irish pub

Mom: oh, and here i was finally proud of you…

AUTHOR NOTE:
Really? She was proud of the $83 of condoms?

HOW LONG DOES IT TAKE YOU TO TEXT?

Mom: are you done cleaning your room?

Me: haha how long does it take you to text?

Mom: as long as it takes you to clean your room

MONEY ON THIS...

Me: Mom, you have money on this? That I won't finish college?

Mom: No way! I lost a fortune when you finished high school!

PURPLE M&M'S

Me: Wow mom, guess what! They have purple M&M's now!

Mom: looks like red and blue had a hell of a time ;)

PICK-UP ORDER

Me: Mom i need you to pick up my birth control

Mom: or you could just stop having sex!

Mom: oh yea my daughter is a whore!

DATING SITES

Mom

I have a date 2night with a guy I found on a dating site

Did his profile say he was a serial killer or rapist?

CHRISTMAS HOTEL

Me: I'll move back in on wednesday and stay until the day after christmas

Mom: Oh, you think so? We're having a special too, buy four nights get the fifth one free

SPANISH CLASSES

Me: I think she's studying hotel management.

Mom: So she's just taking Spanish classes?

YELLOW SUV

Mom: Honey we haven't heard from you in a few days and I just saw in the police log that an unidentified male driving a yellow SUV hit a girl and drove away. If it was you don't worry she wasn't hurt you can come home!

Me: Mom I'm still at the beach... Why would you assume its me?

Mom: well it wouldn't be the first person you've hit... plus what other male do you know who drives a yellow SUV?

TEEN PICTURES

FROM MOM:

awwww such nice teen pictures...and none of you are pregnant!!!

YOU HAVE TO PICK ONE OR THE OTHER

Me: Would you love me if I was gay?

Mom: Yes of course. You're my daughter, I will always love you.

Me: What if I was a bi-sexual

Mom: No, because then you're a slut. You have to pick one or the other.

CUSTODY OF THE KIDS

FROM MOM:

The reason your dad and I never divorced is that neither of us wanted custody of the kids

VODKA TONICS

Mom: There is something wrong with you.

Me: You had me.

Mom: No, I'm pretty sure your father did and I didn't have anything to do with it.

Me: What???

Mom: Too many vodka tonics.

HALF PLANNED

Me: I was an accident wasn't I?

Mom: No you were half planned. I wanted a baby and your father didn't know that I stopped taking the pill.

BLOOD TYPE

Me: What type of blood do i have?

Mom: Red

RED HAIR

Mom: You're the one with red hair.

Me: What's that supposed to mean?

Mom: You have no soul…

BRITISH ACCENT

Mum

Me: These Americans are in love with my British accent.

Mum: If Americans like our accents so much, why didn't they keep them?

Send

PHONE COVER

Me: My phone is falling apart. The cover on the keyboard came off...

Mom: Don't have unprotected text

TROLL MOM

Me: Make me a sandwich

Mom: POOF! you're a sandwich!

OUT OF BED

FROM MOM:

I hope you had to get up out of bed and walk across your room to check this text message

SMALL SIZE

Me: That is NOT what I ordered. Its the small size. Im not eating it.

Mom: Is that the same reason you broke up with your boyfriend?

BLAME IT ON MOM!

Me: I bombed my exam :(

Mom: Imagine how much smarter you'd be if i didn't drink when I was pregnant with you.

MOM'S FIRST TEXT

AUTHOR NOTE:
And here is the award for best first text EVER!

CARD GAME

Mom: So honey one of the women I play cards with has a gay son as well. Would you like us to hook you up?

Me: What! Im not gay!!

Mom: Then why are you in nursing school?

ACCIDENT

Mom: Did you spill ice on the floor?

Me: It was an accident

Mom: So were you

LOVE

Me: You know you love me

Mom: No, first you were a pain in my vagina, now your a pain in my ass

KITTY CAT BIRTH CONTROL

Me: reaaally cool. my cat ate my birth control.

Mom: You're supposed to swallow it, not put it in your pussy.

CHEESECAKE

Me: can I have a bite of your cheesecake in the fridge?

Mom: No, Stop asking. I gave you life, now leave me alone.

SNEAK OUT

FROM MOM:

Next time you sneak out, I suggest not letting your friends upload and tag you in pictures on Facebook of the night before. Idiot. -Love Mom

GRANDMA

Me: Why did you give me a car deodorizer for Christmas?

Gma: To cover up the smell of pot...

WANKETS

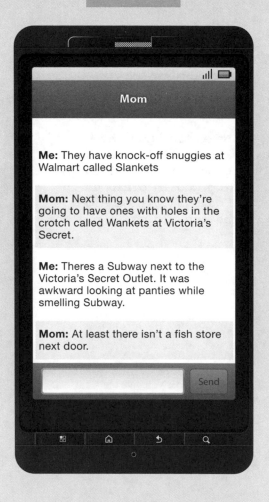

Mom

Me: They have knock-off snuggies at Walmart called Slankets

Mom: Next thing you know they're going to have ones with holes in the crotch called Wankets at Victoria's Secret.

Me: Theres a Subway next to the Victoria's Secret Outlet. It was awkward looking at panties while smelling Subway.

Mom: At least there isn't a fish store next door.

Send

RICH NUGGETS

FROM MOM:

You should never delete my texts. Each one is filled with rich nuggets of wisdom. Someday you can compile them into a book and sell it and make millions.

GUYS ARE VERY CURIOUS

Mom: Tell your boyfriend all about your period. Guys are very curious about it, but too afraid to ask.

Me: Are you trying to get him to dump me???

Mom: You know I don't like him.

PREGNANT

Me: I joined the Harry Potter alliance!

Mom: I guess I don't have to worry about you getting pregnant

THE REASON I HAD YOU

FROM MOM:

I only had you so I could laugh at you.

COLLEGE EDUCATED

Me: John called me a stupid bitch

Mom: Actually tell him you graduated from college so that makes you a well educated bitch.

A GHOST

Mom: We have a ghost.

Me: What do you want me to do about it? Call an exorcist?

Mom: No. Call Weight Watchers. Bastard ate my brownie.

PUT DOWN THE...

Me: I love you

Mom: Put down the vodka

AUTHOR NOTE:
May or not have received the same type of text a few times in college. Except it was phrased "Put the whiskey down."

SAY IT TOGETHER

FROM MOM:

Just Had a client come in the office by the name Sue Lutt. Say it together...I laughed too.

AMERICAN WAY

Me: I'm asian, and I suck at math!

Mom: that's because you are learning it the American way.

CHANGED HIS MIND

FROM MOM:

Dad said no, but I looked at him like this -_- and he changed his mind.

APPLE JUICE

FROM MOM:

I spilled apple juice
on my Iphone. How
appropriate

NO FEET

Mom: If you had no feet, would you still wear shoes?

Me: No of course not, why?

Mom: You have no boobs, Then why do u still wear a bra?

LEARN FROM YOUR MISTAKES

Me: Ha ha ha! You should learn from your mistakes.

Mom: Yeah, that's why I only had one kid.

➡ **phase 7:**
equals at long last

They taught us to walk, we taught them to walk their finger across a Touch-Tone keypad. They hated discovering our sexuality, we hated discovering theirs through text. We tried to make it up to them with grades, they tried to make it up to us through advice. We insulted them in high school, they owned us through text. It's a natural progression, as old as time...or at least as old as the cell phone.

It was only inevitable that at some point, apparently in the seventh phase, we would once again become equals on all fronts. Sure, Mom and Dad kept slinging dirt at us through text, but we recovered enough from the shock of it all to fire back and retaliate. Plus, we learned a thing or two from ol' Ma and Pa about how to really stick it to someone, and we weren't afraid to show them how well they'd taught us.

Now we are in textual maturity, where both parties are adept at texting and insulting each other. Now the laughs come from a friendly banter that showcases the cleverness of both parent and child. Once and for all, we are true friends who insult each other and point out our inadequacies. Because that's what true friends do right? Here's the best of the best back and forth.

WELL GOOD MORNING TO YOU TOO...

Me: Good morning birthgiver

Mom: Good morning after sex results

LEAVE BAIL MONEY

Me: What's for dinner?

Mom: Well, I was gonna make tacos but...I might be going to jail cause I'm about to kill your sister.

Me: Alright, I'll bail you out, leave money.

NAME CHANGE

Dad: You need to change your name...

Me: Um...why Dad?

Dad: cuz Kyle is a dick name

Me: Didn't you name me that?

SNIFFER

Me: Dad, why do you smell like weed?

Dad: Why does your nose work so good?

FISHING

Mom: Ur father took me fishin for the first time! put the worm on the hook by myself!

Me: LOL good going mom

Mom: I'm a pro! Just call me a master baiter!

Me: LMAO read that out loud mom!

Mom: I don't get it what's funny?

Me: Oh mom... >.<

MOM LOVES KE$HA

Me: Mom! I got an A on my math test!

Mom: U runnin this town just lyk a klub.

Me: No you don't wanna mess with us, got jesus on my neck-a-lus-us-us.

TRUCK STOP

Me: I'm watching a show about sex trafficking. Please don't bang prostitutes at truck stops.

Dad: Are BJ's ok?

SOMETHING FOR ME

Me: Okay, dad. Thanks for lending me the money.

Dad: Okay. Now that I've done something for you, you need to do something for me.

Me: Of course!

Dad: Have you heard of farmville?

THAT'S CREATIVE

Me: What are you guys doing tonight?

Mom: Sex...painting

Me: Well that's creative.

Mom: i meant it as a joke as if me and ur father ever have sex.

KNOW WHAT'S AWKWARD?

Dad

Do you know what's awkward?

What?

When GPS tells a gay person to go straight.

Haha I thought GPS would tell them to go south

PRICELESS

Dad: Attempting to help ur brother w/ art hw without much success.

Me: Just take a pic to kinkos copy it and then trace it

Dad: I was able to use the copy machine in office. Getting an A in art....PRICELESS

FIERY PIT

Me: I did yard work all day today and the back yard looks great!! I really hope the world does not end today, I want to enjoy our new fire-pit!

Dad: O honey its not like you will be going anywhere but a fiery pit if the world does end.

"SH" WORDS

Dad: shirt, shower, ship, shin...I just love "sh" words

Me: Here's one..."SHHHH!"

ISN'T DAD THERE?

Mom: Come downstairs and talk to me please I'm lonely

Me: Isn't Dad there?

Mom: Yes but I like you more

SNICKERS

Dad: Is your mother on her way?!

Me: Yeah…why?

Dad: I need to hide the snickers!

MARDI GRAS!

Mom: In New Orleans! Lots of college kids.

Me: Make sure you keep your pants on…

Mom: I will keep my pants on, but I can't make any promises about my top!

SAY NO TO CRACK

Dad: Charlie Sheen needs to learn how to say no to crack

Me: Yea, and the hookers

Dad: That's the type of crack I meant (_|_)

DINNER DATE

Me: Aw, how cute, you took mom on a dinner date. Does it come with flowers?

Dad: No just lots of sex.

Me: Um, wow

Dad: Now that's an image you won't forget ;)

Mom: Did you get the card I sent you?

Me: Yes

Mom: Was there money in it?

Me: Yeah I already used it to buy condoms, hookers, booze and a shit ton of coke

Mom: Don't do drugs on Valentine's Day

NUDISTS

Me: Mom...can we become nudists?

Mom: Have you seen me naked? ...Do you REALLY want that?

I WAS UNTIL I HAD YOU

Me: What's up?

Mom: Your dad is taking a nap. I made sure I tired him out first...

Me: OH. Ewwwwwww.

Mom: What?! We talk about your sex life!

Me: That's because I'm young and attractive.

Mom: I was until I had you.

COOKWARE

Me: I just found a way to pay my rent. I'm going to start growing and selling pot.

Dad: Your 8 year old sister wants to know what that means.

Me: I'm going to start manufacturing and distributing cookware

Dad: Well played son

SQUEEZE HER

Dad: Are you with her right now?

Me: yea

Dad: Make sure you squeeze her left boob for me :>)

Me: Why? her right one is bigger

Dad: LoL, you are my son

TOO OLD OR TOO MUCH?

Mom: Do u think a clit piercing is nasty?

Me: Not really. But I am considerably younger than you.

Mom: meaning what. I'm too old to get one?

DANCING WITH THE STARS

Mom: I like Chris Brown ;)

Me: He's just so 2006

Mom: but he sang in 2011...

Me: I know. I know his music, but he's just not very "in" right now

Mom: That explains it. He was singing on Dancing with the Stars. AND his pants were up.

ALL YOU EVER CALL FOR...

Me: Can I borrow 50 bucks?

Mom: You dont call to say hi, you didnt call on my birthday, all you ever call for is money!

Me: 40 bucks?

Mom: Ok.

UNIV OF PINK

Mom: Do you have some red panties that say Univ of Pink?

Me: Yes! They are my favorite!

Mom: Good! I found them in the couch. I was worried Dad was having a fling w/ some ho.

CINDERELLA

Dad: We made it. But i tell you this getting picked up by a limo has got to stop its going right to my head.

Me: hopefully you have strings to keep your heads from floating away after all this high rollery.

Dad: Did you say something? Please speak to my servants.

Me: im changing my name to Cinderella.

Dad: Does that make me the king?

Me: No she was an orphan.

LISTENING TO JUSTIN BIEBER

Dad: Are you listening to Justin Bieber?

Me: No Dad, I'm watching porn.

Dad: Atta Boy!

GOOD CHILD

Me: Im celebrating my black sheep status in this family as the only unmarried childless one, with a beer on my lunch break!

Dad: Jokes on you. That makes you the good child

ANNIVERSARY

Me: When is your and dad's anniversary?

Mom: June 4th 1988 (i think) will be 22 this year? are you trying to see if i was pregnant when i got married?

Me: No I was just wondering when you guys will hit the 25 year mark

Mom: Oh.

FLAT WALLET

Me: I was accepted to University!

Dad: My wallet feels flatter already...

Me: It's better for your hips, there was too much in there anyway.

SLEEP WALKING

Dad: Did you know you were sleep walking last night?

Me: I was? What was I doing?

Dad: Humping the bathtub.

MOTHER-DAUGHTER HOUSE

Mom: When I get old, can you buy a mother-daughter house so I can move in?

Me: Mom, can I move out of YOUR house first?

CHILDLINE

Me: Hey Dad!

Dad: Stop bothering me, IT'S BLOODY 2AM!

Me: Wanted to make sure you were awake for work ;)

Dad: You're dead

Me: I'm calling Childline

WATCH OUT FOR DRAGONS

Dad: Watch out for dragons

Me: What?

Dad: Dragons are eating up all the virgins up in here.

Me: haha. Well I'm safe.

Dad: Really, thats disappointing. Mom called you a bitch.

DON'T TELL YOUR BROTHER

MUGGLES

Me: We're at the mall.

Mom: With your friends?

Me: No, with Voldemort.

Mom: Oh my. Plz be careful. I heard he's killing quite a bit of muggles these days.

THE HOLY GRAIL

Mom: Hey, I've looked through all of our movies, but I still can't find the Holy Grail...do you know where it is?

Me: I have no idea, but I hear they've been looking for a few centuries, so good luck with that...

MOLESTING THE MAZDA

Me: Your car alarm is going off. I must have sat on the keys.

Dad: Make sure no houligans are molesting the Mazda.

Me: The car's fine....

TWILIGHT MOM

Mom: Hey I bought you an Edward vposter for your dorm room. Originally I was holding two posters, an Edward one for you and a Jacob one for me but then your brother asked me why I had two and I couldnt justify buying it for my sewing room.

Me: Thanks, and about the one for you...you do realize that he's like 17 right? That would make you a cradlerobber.

Mom: Actually, hes over 100 years old. That makes you a gold digger. P.S. I prefer the term cougar. :-P

THE JACKSON FIVE

Me: I'll be there

Mom: Thanks Michael

Me: You're welcome Janet

Mom: Oops, my boob popped out! Wardrobe malfunction!

NICKLEBAGS

Mom: your dad wants to know if you can bring him home a nicklebag from your drug dealer. sorry hes in that mood again

Me: it's not the 70s anymore, they don't sell nicklebags.

NURSING HOME

Dad: You're such a bitch sometimes.

Me: Watch it old man, Im all that stands between you and a nursing home one day.

AUTHOR NOTE:
Growing up I know that I always joked about sending my dad to a nursing home.

FROM THE BEYOND

Me: Im dead

Mom: So you are talking to me from the beyond?

Me: No mom hungover

BOTH CALLED OUT!

Dad

Me: Hey!

Dad: Aren't you supposed to be at school?

Me: Aren't you supposed to be at work?

Dad: Touche…

Send

SECOND BASE

Me: I'm watching the doctor get to second base with mom.

Dad: How do you know about the bases? Did you google it?

Me: He's touching her boobs

Dad: Damn, maybe he should pitch in on dinner.

HUNGRY, HUNGRY, HOBOS

FROM MOM:

I saw a hobo on the side of the road with a sign that said "hungry hungry hobo." I couldn't stop laughing

SAVED

Me: (mass message) Hey guys, its Jenn, this is my new number, Save this shit!!

Dad: The shit has been saved!

BUTTLESS

Mom: If you don't stop I will unscrew your belly button and your butt will fall off!

Me: Mom im not five anymore

WAKE UP

Dad: Wake up, its time to go to school!

Me: ...I'm gonna cause you a slow painful death

Dad: I've already married your mother.

WATCH YOUR LANGUAGE

Dad: Fuck

Me: Watch your language

Dad: Fornicate

GAS STATION

FROM DAD:

I am at the gas station and there is a whole Amish family here I'm not sure why the Amish need gas but I think it's worth investigating

LIKE FATHER, LIKE DAUGHTER

Dad: What kind of bees make milk?

Me: B-cups?

Dad: No damnit, boo-BEES

Me: Why does Ariel wear seashells?

Dad: Why?

Me: Cause she doesn't fit into D-shells

Dad: You're definitely my child

SUPER EXTRA SMALL

Dad: Hey son, I bought you some super extra small condoms :)

Me: Dad, you do realize I inherit that stuff from you, right?

Dad: So like I was saying, I got you some extra large condoms. Come pick them up later, okay?

HANDCUFFS

Me: They were Toy handcuffs.

Mom: Well I don't know anything about toy handcuffs! I only had the real ones ;)

Me: Mom do not wink at me.

FOREVER YOUNG

Me: Happy 49th DAD! I love you so much!

Dad: Its 48! YOU RUINED MY DAY :(

EPIC FAIL

Mom: how was the poop?

Me: what?

Mom: oops :) hehe i meant pool.

Me: EPIC FAIL!!

Mom: yeah and so was your dads condom...

BAD DRIVER

Mom

Me: You do not help the stereotype of women drivers.

Mom: I'm not a bad driver, I just like giving the gift of near-death experiences.

Send

GOOD GIRL

Me: You will like her she is a good girl!

Dad: There is no such thing as a "good girl," just bitches who know how to lie.

UNLIKE UR MOTHER

Dad: You out tonight?

Me: i aaaam!

Dad: Please keep your legs closed, unlike your mother…

Me: hahaha dad!!

GOOD NEWS!

Me: Hey I have some good news.

Mom: You finally got laid?

Me: No...I got into college.

Mom: Oh, that's nice.

ARE YOU SURE?

Me: Mom, some chick said I might be the father of her kid.

Mom: Are you?

Me: No, I never slept with her.

Mom: Are you sure? You are a boy.

Me: ...I'm not a slut, ma.

NEW PAPER BAG

Dad: Big sunglasses are the new paper bag? You can't tell who has an ugly face...

Me: and they're way easier to convince girls to wear during sex.

10 A.M. ON A GAMEDAY

Dad: The fact that its 10am on a gameday and I have yet to shotgun is absurd.

Me: Dad you are NOT in college anymore.

 **"bonus texts"**

CHANGED MY MIND

Me: I'm just staying here another night, I'll be home tomorrow sometime.

Me: Changed my mind, can you come get me?

Dad: I changed my mind when we brought you home but it was too late then. Just stand on the highway and someone nice will pick you up… maybe they will even keep you. Fingers crossed. good luck

dad someones trying to break in! i think they shot the dog!!!!

i'm at denny's...let me know what happens

SILENT TREATMENT

FROM MOM:

Tell your father i'm giving him the silent treatment until he learns to put the toilet seat down. I fell in the toilet this morning!!!

TESTED

FROM DAD:

I had a dream last night that I had sex with Snooki....without a condom. Should I go get tested?

Y U NO ANSWER?

Mom: Why didn't you answer me when I called you?!

Me: Because I was in the middle of Government class...?

Mom: And?

SPRING BREAK

Me: I'll be home soon.

Mom: excited 4 spring break . practicing my fist pump. don't text me.

DOOR PROBLEMS

Dad: I hate it when you try to open a door as fast as you're walking and you end up slamming into it.

Me: OMG! U ok?!

Dad: I'm fine. almost died of laughter though. It was your mom that walked into the door and she tried to play it off.

• • •

Mom: (15 mins later) Honey, you'll need to find a ride home from school, I have a major migraine.

Dad

Me: I am almost to the bottom of my 2nd gallon of milk this week

Dad: U will turn in 2 a cow

Me: Was that a fat joke?

Dad: Moo

Me: Hahah I need to start submitting our conversations online

Dad: That's udderly ridiculous!

Send

BLENDERS

Dad: You're going to love what we got you for christmas this year.

Me: Is it another blender?

Dad: What? Wait, didn't we get you one last year too?

Me: Yeah

Dad: Shit.

DIAGON ALLEY

Mom: I wasn't really that drunk...

Me: You crouched in the fireplace, grabbed some ashes and yelled "Diagon Alley"...

➡ conclusion

So, where do we go from here? Well, the answer is simple: holographs. Yes, you heard us. Holographs.

Time moves fast ladies and gentlemen. Just like the technology is going to move at lightning speed, so too will our time as the "kids" in the parent-kid relationship. Pretty soon, we'll be the parents, sending holographs where our old, wrinkled face is going to be hovering ten inches in front of our kids' faces yelling, "Honey, I don't know if I did this right! How do I know if it's working?"

So remember how awkward it was when you got those "sexts" from your parents? Well, imagine sending one to your child, but in holographic form. Yeah, be careful with that Send button ladies and gentlemen, because the future of awkward parent texts has just started!

➡ acknowledgments

Mac Mackie from Old North Agency has been the best agent one could ask for. He has helped and advised us throughout the whole process of writing this book. His ideas and enthusiasm have made a big impact on us!

Amanda Taylor from Charlotte, NC, not only are you a great friend, you have also been a wonderful help picking out some of the funniest texts for the book and the site. We are glad to have you working with us!

Mom and Dad, thanks for being so supportive our whole lives. You guys really are great parents!

A big thanks to the whole Sourcebooks team for all your hard work on the book! You guys have made this book possible!

We would also like to give a shout out to our fans of crazythingsparentstext.com! We have had a fantastic time reading the crazy texts that you have submitted. Keep them coming!